James Whitcomb Riley

Sketches in prose

Jamesy - A Christmas story - and others

James Whitcomb Riley

Sketches in prose

Jamesy - A Christmas story - and others

ISBN/EAN: 9783741192333

Manufactured in Europe, USA, Canada, Australia, Japa

Cover: Foto ©Andreas Hilbeck / pixelio.de

Manufactured and distributed by brebook publishing software (www.brebook.com)

James Whitcomb Riley

Sketches in prose

THE WORKS OF JAMES WHITCOMB RILEY ✒ ✒
VOL. II

THE POEMS AND PROSE SKETCHES OF JAMES WHITCOMB RILEY

SKETCHES IN PROSE JAMESY—A CHRISTMAS STORY—AND OTHERS

CHARLES SCRIBNER'S SONS NEW YORK 1899

Copyright, 1891, 1897, by
JAMES WHITCOMB RILEY

⁎ *The publication of this Homestead Edition of the works of James Whitcomb Riley is made possible by the courtesy of The Bowen-Merrill Company, of Indianapolis, the original publishers of Mr. Riley's books.*

TO
UNCLE MART

CONTENTS

	PAGE
God Bless us Every One .	2
JAMESY—A CHRISTMAS STORY .	3
AN ADJUSTABLE LUNATIC .	43
TOD	69
A REMARKABLE MAN	91
A NEST-EGG . .	117
TALE OF A SPIDER . . .	131
WHERE IS MARY ALICE SMITH?	167
ECCENTRIC MR. CLARK .	183
"THE BOY FROM ZEENY" .	209
THE OLD MAN	229

JAMESY
A CHRISTMAS STORY

GOD BLESS US EVERY ONE

"God bless us every one!" prayed Tiny Tim,
    Crippled, and dwarfed of body, yet so tall
Of soul, we tiptoe earth to look on him,
        High towering over all.

He loved the loveless world, nor dreamed indeed
    That it, at best, could give to him, the while,
But pitying glances, when his only need
        Was but a cheery smile.

And thus he prayed, "God bless us every one!"—
    Enfolding all the creeds within the span
Of his child-heart; and so, despising none,
        Was nearer saint than man.

I like to fancy God, in Paradise,
    Lifting a finger o'er the rhythmic swing
Of chiming harp and song, with eager eyes
        Turned earthward, listening—

The Anthem stilled—the Angels leaning there
    Above the golden walls—the morning sun
Of Christmas bursting flower-like with the prayer,
        "God bless us every one!"

JAMESY

One week ago this Christmas day, in the little back office that adjoins the counting-room of the "Daily Journal," I sat in genial conversation with two friends. I do not now recall the theme of our discussion, but the general trend of it—suggested, doubtless, by the busy scene upon the streets—I remember most distinctly savored of the mellowing influences of the coming holidays, with perhaps an acrid tang of irony as we dwelt upon the great needs of the poor at such a time, and the chariness with which the hand of opulence was wont to dole out alms. But for all that we were merry, and as from time to time our glances fell upon the ever-shifting scene outside, our hearts grew warmer, and within the eyes the old dreams glimmered into fuller dawn. It was during a lull of conversation, and while the philanthropic mind, perchance, was wandering amid the outer throng, and doubtless quoting to itself "Whene'er I take my walks abroad," that our privacy was abruptly broken into by the grimy apparition of a boy of ten; a ragged little fellow —not the stereotyped edition of the street-waif, but a cross between the boot-black and the infantine Italian with the violin. Where he had entered, and how, would have puzzled us to answer; but there he stood before us, as it were, in a majesty of insignificance. I have never had the features of a boy impress me as did his, and as I stole a covert glance at my companions I was pleased to find the evidence of more than ordinary interest in their faces. They gazed in attentive silence on the little fellow, as, with uncovered, frowzy head, he stepped boldly forward, yet with an air of deference as unlooked for as becoming.

"I don't want to bother you gentlemens," he began, in a frank but hesitating tone that rippled hurriedly along as he marked a general nod of indulgence for the interruption. "I don't want to bother nobody, but if I can raise fifty cents—and I've got a nickel—and if I can raise the rest—and it ain't much, you know—on'y forty-five—and if I can raise the rest—I tell you, gentlemens," he broke off abruptly, and speaking with italicized sincerity, "I want jist fifty cents, 'cause I can git a blackin'-box fer that, and brush and ever'thing, and you can bet if I had *that* I wouldn't haf to ast nobody fer nothin'!

JAMESY

And I ain't got no father ner mother, ner brother ner—ner—no sisters, neether; but that don't make no difference, 'cause I'll work—at *anything*—yes, sir—when I can git anything to do—and I sleep jist any place—and I ain't had no breakfast—and, honest, gentlemens, I'm a good boy—I don't swear ner smoke ner chew—but that's all right—on'y if you'll——jist make up forty-five between you—and that's on'y fifteen cents apiece—I'll thank you, I will, and I'll jist do anything—and it's coming Christmas, and I'll roll in the nickels, don't you fergit—if I on'y got a box—'cause I throw up a 'bad' shine!—and I can git the box fer fifty cents if you gentlemens'll on'y make up forty-five between you." At the conclusion of this long and rambling appeal, the little fellow stood waiting with an eager face for a response.

A look of stoical deliberation played about the features of the oldest member of the group, as with an air of seriousness, which, I think, even the boy recognized as affected, he asked:

"And you couldn't get a box like that for—say forty cents? Fifty cents looks like a lot of money to lay out in the purchase of a blacking-box."

The boy smiled wisely as he answered:

"Yes, it might look big to a feller that ain't up on prices, but *I* think it's *cheap*, 'cause it's a second-hand box, and a *new* one would cost seventy-five cents anyhow—'thout no brushes ner nothin'!"

In the meantime I had dropped into the little fellow's palm the only coin I had in my possession, and we all laughed as he closed his thanks with: "Oh, come, Cap, go the *other* nickel, er I won't git out o' here with *half* enough!" and at that he turned to the former speaker.

"Well, really," said that gentleman, fumbling in his pockets, "I don't believe I've got a dime with me."

"A *dime*," said the little fellow, with a look of feigned compassion. "Ain't got a dime? Maybe I'd loan you *this* one!" And we all laughed again.

"Tell you what do now," said the boy, taking advantage of the moment, and looking coaxingly into the smiling eyes of the gentleman still fumbling vainly in his pockets.—"Tell you what do: you borry twenty cents of the man that stays behind the counter there, and then we'll go the other fifteen, and that'll make it, and I'll skip out o' here a little the flyest boy you ever see! What do ye soy?" And the little fellow struck a Pat Rooney attitude that would have driven the original inventor mad with envy.

"Give him a quarter!" laughed the gentleman appealed to.

JAMESY

"And here's the other dime," and as the little fellow clutched the money eagerly, he turned; and in a tone of curious gravity, he said:

"Now, honest, gentlemens, I ain't a-givin' you no *game* about the box—'cause a new one costs seventy-five cents, and the one I've got—I mean the one I'm a-goin' to git—is jist as *good* as a new one, on'y it's *second-hand;* and I'm much oblige', gentlemens—honest, I am—and if ever I give you a shine you can jist bet it don't cost you nothin'!"

And with this expression of his gratitude, the little fellow vanished as mysteriously as he had at first appeared.

"That boy hasn't a bad face," said the first speaker—"wide between the eyes—full forehead—good mouth, denoting firmness—altogether, a good, square face."

"And a noble one," said I, perhaps inspired to that rather lofty assertion by the rehearsal of the good points noted by my more observant companion.

"Yes, and an honest, straightforward way of talking, I would say," continued that gentleman. "I only noted one thing to shake my faith in that particular, and that was in his latest reference to the box. You'll remember his saying he was 'giving us no game' about it, whereas he had not been accused of such a thing."

"Oh, he meant about the price, don't you remember?" said I.

"No," said the gentleman at the counter, "you're both wrong. He only threw in that remark because he thought I suspected him, for he recognized me just the instant before that speech, and it confused him, and with some reason, as you will see:—On my way to supper only last night, I overtook that same little fellow in charge of an old man who was in a deplorable state of drunkenness; and you know how slippery the streets were. I think if that old man fell a single time he fell a dozen, and once so violently that I ran to his assistance and helped him to his feet. I thought him badly hurt at first, for he gashed his forehead as he fell, and I helped the little fellow to take him into a drug-store, where the wound, upon examination, proved to be nothing more serious than to require a strip of plaster. I got a good look at the boy, there, however, and questioned him a little; and he said the man was his father, and he was taking him home; and I gathered further from his talk that the man was a confirmed inebriate. Now you'll remember the boy told us here a while ago he had no father, and when he recognized me a moment since and found himself caught in one 'yarn,' at least, he very naturally supposed I would think his entire story a fabrication, hence the suspicious nature of his last remarks, and the sudden transition of his manner from that of real delight to gravity, which change, in my opinion, rather denotes lying to be a new thing to him. I can't be mistaken in the boy, for I noticed, as he turned to go, a bald place on the back of his head, the left side, a 'trade-mark,' first discovered last evening, as he bent over the prostrate form of his father."

"I noticed a thin spot in his hair," said I, "and wondered at the time what caused it."

"And don't you know?"

I shook my head.

"Coal-bins and entry floors.—That little fellow hasn't slept within a bed for years, perhaps."

"But he told you, as you say, last night, he was taking the old man home?"

"Yes, home! I can imagine that boy's home. There are myriads like it in the city here—a cellar or a shed—a box-car or a loft in some old shop, with a father to chase him from it in his sober interludes, and to hold him from it in unconscious shame when helplessly drunk. 'Home, Sweet Home!' That boy has heard it on the hand-organ, perhaps, but never in his heart—you couldn't grind it out of there with a thousand cranks."

The remainder of that day eluded me somehow; I don't know how or where it passed. I suppose it just dropped into a comatose condition, and so slipped away "unknelled, uncoffined, and unknown."

But one clear memory survives—an experience so vividly imprinted on my mind that I now recall its every detail: Entering the Union Depot that evening to meet the train that was to carry me away at six o'clock, muffled closely in my overcoat, yet more closely muffled in my gloomy thoughts, I was rather abruptly stopped by a small boy with the cry of: "Here, you man with the cigar; don't you want them boots blacked? Shine 'em fer ten cents! Shine 'em fer a nickel—on'y you mustn't give me away on that," he added, dropping on his knees near the entrance, and motioning me to set my foot upon the box.

It was then too dark for me to see his face clearly, but I had recognized the voice the instant he had spoken, and had paused and looked around.

"Oh, you'll have plenty o' time," he urged, guessing at the cause of my apparent hesitation. "None o' the trains on time to-night—on'y the Panhandle, and she's jist a-backin' in—won't start fer thirty minutes," and he again beckoned, and rattled a seductive tattoo on the side of his box.

"Well," said I, with a compromising air, "come inside, then, out of the cold."

JAMESY

"'Ginst the rules—cops won't have it. They jist fired me out o' there not ten minutes ago. Oh, come, Cap; step out here; it won't take two minutes," and the little fellow spat professionally upon his brush, with a covert glance of pleasure as he noted the apparent success of the manœuvre. "You don't *live* here, I'll bet," said the boy, setting the first boot on the box, and pausing to blow his hands.

"How do you know that? Did you never see me here before?"

"No, I never *see* you here before, but that ain't no reason. I can tell you don't live here by them shoes— 'cause they've been put up in some little pennyroyal shop, —that's how. When you want a 'fly' shoe you want to git her put up somers where they know somepin' about style. They's good enough *metal* in that shoe, on'y she's about two years off in *style*."

"You're posted, then, in shoes," said I, with a laugh.

"I ort to be," he went on, pantingly, a brush in either hand gyrating with a velocity that jostled his hat over his eyes, leaving most plainly exposed to my investigative eye the "trade-mark" before alluded to; "I ort to be posted in shoes, 'cause I ain't done nothin' but black 'em fer five years."

"You're an old hand, then, at the business," said I.

"I didn't know but maybe you were just starting out. What's an outfit like that worth?"

"Thinkin' o' startin' up?" he asked, facetiously.

"Oh, no," said I, good-humoredly. "I just asked out of idle curiosity. That's a new box, ain't it?"

"*New!*" he repeated with a laugh. "Put up that other hoof. *New?* W'y, if that box had ever had eyes like a human it would a-been a-wearin' specs by this time; that's a old, bald-headed box, with one foot in the grave."

"And what did the old fellow cost you?" I asked, highly amused at the quaint expressions of the boy.

"Cost? Cost nothin'—on'y about a' hour's work. I made that box myse'f, 'bout four year ago."

"Ah!' said I.

"Yes," he went on, "they don't cost nothin'; the boys makes 'em out o' other boxes, you know. Some of 'em gits 'em made, but they ain't no good—ain't no better'n this kind."

"So that didn't cost you anything?" said I, "though I suspect you wouldn't like to part with it for less than —well, I don't know how much money to say—seventy-five cents maybe—would anything less than seventy-five cents buy it?" I craftily interrogated.

"Seventy-five cents! W'y, what's the matter with

you, man? I could git a cart-load of 'em fer seventy-five cents. I'll take yer measure fer one like it fer fifteen, too quick!" and the little fellow leaned back from his work and laughed up in my face with absolute derision.

I pulled my hat more closely down for fear of recognition, but was reassured a moment later as he went on:

"Wisht you lived here; you'd be old fruit fer us fellows. I can see you now a-takin' wind—and we'd give it to you mighty slick now, don't you fergit!" and as the boy renewed his work, I think his little, ragged body shook less with industry than mirth.

"Wisht I'd struck you 'bout ten o'clock this morning!" and, as he spoke, he paused again and looked up in my face with real regret. "Oh, you'd a-been the loveliest sucker of 'em all! W'y, you'd a-went the whole pot yerse'f!"

"How do you mean?" said I, dropping the cigar I held.

"How do I mean? Oh, you don't want to smoke this thing again after it's a-rollin' round here in the dirt!"

"Why, you don't smoke," said I, still reaching for the cigar he held behind him.

"*Me?* Oh, what you givin' me?"

"Come, let me have it," I said, sharply, drawing a case from my pocket and taking out another cigar.

JAMESY

"Oh, you want a *light*," he said, handing me the stub and watching me wistfully. "Couldn't give us a fresh cigar, could you, Cap?"

"I don't know," said I, as though deliberating on the matter. "What was that you were going to tell me just now? You started to tell me what a 'lovely sucker' I'd have been had you met me this morning. How did you mean?"

"Give me a cigar and I'll tell you. Oh, come, now, Cap; give me a smoker and I'll give you the whole game. I will, now, honest!"

I held out the open case.

"Nothin' mean about you, is they?" he said, eagerly taking a fresh cigar in one hand and the stub in the other. "A ten-center, too—*oh, I guess not!*" But, to my surprise, he took the stub between his lips, and began opening his coat. "Guess I'll jist fat this daisy, and save 'er up for Christmas. No, I won't, eether," he broke in suddenly, with a bright, keen flash of second thought. "Tell you what I'll do," holding up the cigar and gazing at it admiringly; "she's a ten-center, ain't she?"

I nodded.

"And worth every cent of it, too, ain't she?"

"Every cent of it," I repeated.

"Then give me a nickel, and she's yourn—'cause if you

can afford to *give* this to me fer nothin', looks like I ort to let you have it fer half-price"; and as I laughingly dropped the nickel in his hand he concluded, "And they's nothin' mean about me, neether!"

"Now, go on with your story," said I. "How about that 'game' you were 'giving,' this morning?"

"Well, I'll tell you, Cap. Us fellers has got to lay fer ever' nickel, 'cause none of us is bondholders; and they's days and days together when we don't make enough to even starve on.—What I mean is, we on'y make enough to pay fer aggervatin' our appetites with jist about enough chuck to keep us starvin'-hungry. So, you see, when a feller ain't got nothin' else to do, and his appetite won't sleep in the same bunk with him, he's bound to git onto somepin' crooked and git up all sorts o' dodges to git along. Some gives 'em one thing, and some another, but you bet they got to be mighty slick now, 'cause people won't have 'orphans,' and 'fits,' and 'cripples,' and 'drunk fathers,' and 'mothers that eats morphine,' and 'white-swellin',' and 'consumption,' and all that sort o' taffy! Got to git 'er down finer'n that! But *I* been a-gittin' in my work all the same, don't you fergit! You won't ever blow, now?"

"How could I 'blow,' and what if I did?—I don't live here," I replied.

"Well, you better never blow, anyhow; 'cause if ever us duffers would git onto it you'd be a spiled oyster!"

"Go on," said I, with an assuring tone.

"The lay I'm on jist now," he continued, dropping his voice and looking cautiously around, "is a-hidin' my box and a-rushin' in, suddent-like, where they's a crowd o' nobs a-talkin' politics er somepin', and a-jist startin' in, and 'fore they know *what's* a-comin' I'm a-flashin' up a nickel er a dime, and a-tellin' 'em if I on'y had enough more to make fifty cents I could buy a blackin'-box, and wouldn't have to ast no boot o' my grandmother! And two minutes chinnin' does it, don't you see, cause *they* don't know nothin' 'bout blackin'-boxes; they're jist as soft as *you* air. They got an idy, maybe, that blackin'-boxes comes all the way from Chiny, with cokeynut whiskers packed 'round 'em; and I make it solid by a-sayin' I'm on'y goin' to git a *second-hand* box—see? But *that* ain't the pint—it's the Mr. Nickel I' already *got*. Oh! it'll paralyze 'em ever' time! *Some*times fellers'll make up seventy-five cents er a dollar, and tell me to 'git a *new* box, and go into the business right.' That's a thing that always rattles me. Now, if they'd on'y growl a little and look like they was jist a-puttin' up 'cause the first one did, I can stand it; but when they go to pattin' me on the head, and a-tellin' me 'that's right,' and 'not to be afeard o' work,' and I'll 'come out all right,' and a-tellin' me to 'git a good substantial box while I'm a-gittin',' and a-ponyin' up handsome, there's where I weaken—I do, honest!" And never so plainly as at that moment did I see within his face and in his eyes the light of true nobility.

"You see," he went on, in a tone of voice half courage, half apology, "I' got a family on my hands, and I' jist *got* to git along somehow! I could git along on the square deal as long as *mother* was alive—'cause she'd *work* —but ever sence *she* died—and that was winter 'fore last—I've kindo' had to double on the old thing all sorts o' ways. But Sis don't know it. Sis *she* thinks I'm the squarest muldoon in the business," and even side by side with the homely utterance a great sigh faltered from his lips.

"And who is Sis?" I inquired with new interest.

"Sis?" he repeated, knocking my foot from the box, and leaning back, still in the old position, his hat now lying on the ground beside him, and his frowzy hair tossed backward from the full, broad brow—"Who's Sis?" he repeated with an upward smile that almost dazzled me—"W'y, Sis is—is—w'y, Sis is the boss girl— and don't you fergit it!"

No need had he to tell me more than this. I knew

JAMESY

who "Sis" was by the light of pride in the uplifted eyes; I knew who "Sis" was by the exultation in the broken voice, and the half-defiant tossing of the frowzy head; I knew who "Sis" was by the little, naked hands thrown upward openly; I knew who "Sis" was by the tear that dared to trickle through the dirt upon her ragged brother's face. And don't *you* forget it!

O that boy down there upon his knees!—there in the cinders and the dirt—so far, far down beneath us that we trample on his breast and grind our heels into his very heart; O that boy there, with his lifted eyes, and God's own glory shining in his face, has taught me, with an eloquence beyond the trick of mellow-sounding words and metaphor, that love may find a purer home beneath the rags of poverty and vice than in all the great warm heart of Charity.

I hardly knew what impulse prompted me, but as the boy rose to his feet and held his hand out for the compensation for his work, I caught the little dingy palm close, close within my own, and wrung it as I would have wrung the hand of some great conqueror.

The little fellow stared at me in wonderment, and although his lips were silent, I can but believe that had they parted with the utterance within his heart my feelings had received no higher recognition than the old contemptuous phrase, "Oh, what you givin' me?"

"And so you've got a family on your hands?" I inquired, recovering an air of simple curiosity, and toying in my pocket with some bits of change. "How much of a family?"

"On'y three of us now."

"Only three of you, eh? Yourself, and Sis, and— and—"

"The old man," said the boy, uneasily; and after a pause, in which he seemed to swallow an utterance more bitter, he added, "And he ain't no good on earth!"

"Can't work?" I queried.

"*Won't* work," said the boy, bitterly. "He *won't* work—he won't do nothin'—on'y '*budge*'! And I haf to steer him in ever' night, 'cause the cops won't pull him any more—they won't let him in the station-house more'n they'd let him in a parler, 'cause he's a plum goner now, and liable to 'croak' any minute."

"Liable to what?" said I.

"Liable to jist keel over—wink out, you know—'cause he has fits,—kindo' jimjams, I guess. Had a fearful old matinee with him last night! You see he comes all sorts o' games on me, and I haf to put up fer him—'cause he's *got* to have *whiskey*, and if we can on'y keep him about so full he's a regular lamb; but he don't stand no monkeyin' when he wants whiskey, now you bet! Sis can handle him better'n me, but *she's* been a-losin' her grip on him lately—you see Sis ain't stout any more, and been kindo' sick-like so long she humors him, you know, more'n she'd ort. And he couldn't git on his pins at all yisterday morning, and Sis sent fer me, and I took him down a pint, and that set him a-runnin' so that when I left he made Sis give up a quarter he saw me slip her; and it jist happened I run into him that evening and got him in, or he'd a-froze to death. I guess he must a-kindo' had 'em last night, 'cause he was the wildest man you ever see—saw grasshoppers with paper-collars on, and old sows with feather-duster tails—the durndest programme you ever heerd of! And he got so bad onc't he was a-goin' to *belt* Sis, and did *try* it: and—and I had to chug him one or he'd a-done it. And then he cried, and *Sis* cried, and *I* cri—, I— *Dern him!* you can bet yer life *I* didn't cry!" And as the boy spoke, the lips quivered into stern compression, the little hands gripped closer at his side, but for all that the flashing eye grew blurred and the lids dropped downward.

"That's a boss shine on them shoes."

I was mechanically telling over in my hand the three small coins I had drawn from my pocket.

JAMESY

"That *is* a nice job!" said I, gazing with an unusual show of admiration at the work; "and I thought," continued I, with real regret, "that I had two dimes and a nickel here, and was thinking that, as these were Christmas-times, I'd just give you a quarter for your work."

"Honest, Cap?"

"Honest!" I repeated, "but the fact is the two dimes, as I thought they were, are only two three-cent pieces, so I have only eleven cents in change, after all."

"Spect they'd change a bill fer you 'crost there at the lunch-counter," he suggested, with charming artlessness.

"Won't have time—there's my train just coupling.— But take this—I'll see you again sometime, perhaps."

"How big a bill is it you *want* changed?" asked the little fellow, with a most acquisitive expression, and a swift glance at our then lonely surroundings.

"I only have one bill with me," said I, nervously, "and that's a five."

"Well, here then," said the boy, hurriedly, with another and more scrutinizing glance about him—"guess I can 'commodate you." And as I turned in wonder, he drew from some mysterious recess in the lining of his coat a roll of bills, from which he hastily detached four in number, returned the roll; and before I had recovered from my surprise, he had whisked the note from my fingers and left in my hand instead the proper change.

"This is on the dead, now, Cap. Don't you ever cheep about me havin' wealth, you know; 'cause it ain't *mine*— that is, it *is* mine, but I'm a— There goes yer train. Ta-ta!"

"The day before Christmas," said I, snatching his hand, and speaking hurriedly—"the day before Christmas I'm coming back, and if you'll be here when the 5:30 train rolls in you'll find a man that wants his boots blacked— maybe to get married in, or something—anyway he'll want a shine like this, and he'll come prepared to pay the highest market price—do you understand?"

"You jist tell that feller fer me," said the boy, eclipsing the twinkle of one eye, and dropping his voice to an inflection of strictest confidence—"you jist tell that feller fer me that I'm his oyster!"

"And you'll meet him, sure?" said I.

"I will," said the boy. And he kept his word.

My ride home was an incoherent fluttering of the wings of time, in which travail one fretful hour was born, to gasp its first few minutes helplessly; then moan, roll over and kick out its legs and sprawl about; then crawl a little—stagger to its feet and totter on; then tumble down a time or two and knock its empty head against the floor and howl; then loom up awkwardly on gangling legs, too much in their own way to comprehend that they were in the way of everybody else; then limp a little as it worried on—drop down exhausted—moan again—toss up its hands—shriek out, and die in violent convulsions.

We have all had that experience of the car-wheels—had them enter into conversation with us as we gayly embarked upon some pleasant trip, perhaps; had them rattle off in scraps of song, or lightly twit us with some dear one's name, or even go so far as to laugh at us and mock us for some real or fancied dereliction of car-etiquette. I shall ever have good reason to remember how once upon a time a boy of fourteen, though greatly undersized, told the conductor he was only ten, and although the unsuspecting official accepted the statement as a truth, with the proper reduction in the fare, the car-wheels called that boy a "liar" for twenty miles —and twenty miles as long and tedious as he has ever compassed in his journey through this vale of tears.

The car-wheels on this bitter winter evening were not at all communicative. They were sullen and morose. They didn't feel like singing, and they wouldn't laugh. They had no jokes, and if there was one peculiar quality of tone they possessed in any marked degree it was that of sneering. They had a harsh, discordant snarl, as it seemed, and were spiteful and insinuating.

The topic they had chosen for that night's consideration was evidently of a very complex and mysterious nature, and they gnawed and mumbled at it with such fierceness, and, withal, such selfishness, I could only catch a flying fragment of it now and then, and that, I noticed, was of the coarsest fibre of intelligence, and of slangy flavor. Listening with the most painful interest, I at last made out the fact that the inflection seemed to be in the interrogative, and, with anxiety the most intense, I slowly came to comprehend that they were desirous of ascertaining the exact distance between two given points, but the proposition seemed determined not to round into fuller significance than to query mockingly, "How *fur* is it? How *fur* is it? How *fur*, how *fur*, how *fur* is it?" and so on to a most exasperating limit. As this senseless phrase was repeated and reiterated in its growing harshness and unchanging intonation, the relentless pertinacity of the query grew simply agonizing, and when at times the car door opened to admit a brakeman, or the train-boy, who had everything to sell but what I wanted, the emphasized refrain would lift me from my seat and drag me up and down the aisle.

When the phrase did eventually writhe round into form and shade more tangible, my relief was such that I sat down, and in my fancy framed a grim, unlovely tune that suited it, and hummed with it, in an undertone of dismal satisfaction:

> *" How fur—how fur*
> *Is it from here—*
> *From here to Happiness?"*

When I returned, that same refrain rode back into the city with me! All the gay metropolis was robing for the banquet and the ball. All the windows of the crowded thoroughfares were kindling into splendor. Along the streets rode lordly carriages, so weighted down with costly silks, and furs, and twinkling gems, and unknown treasures in unnumbered packages, that one lone ounce of needed charity would have snapped their axles, and a feather's weight of pure benevolence would have splintered every spoke.

And the old refrain rode with me through it all—as stoical, relentless and unchangeable as fate—and in the same depraved and slangy tone in which it seemed to find an especial pride, it sang, and sang again:

> *" How fur—how fur*
> *Is it from here—*
> *From here to Happiness?"*

JAMESY

The train, that for five minutes had been lessening in speed, toiled painfully along, and as I arose impatiently and reached behind me for my overcoat, a cheery voice cried, "Hello, Cap! Want a lift? I'll he'p you with that 'benjamin'"; and as I looked around I saw the grimy features of my little hero of the brush and box.

"Hello!" said I, as much delighted as surprised. "Where did you drop from?"

"Oh, I collared this old hearse a mile er so back yonder," said the little fellow, gayly, standing on the seat behind me and holding up the coat. "Been a-doin' circus-business on the steps out there fer half an hour. You bet I had my eye on *you*, all the same, though!"

"You had, eh?" I exclaimed, gladly, although I instinctively surmised his highest interest in me was centred in my pocket-book. "You had, eh?" I repeated with more earnestness.—"Well, I'm glad of that, Charlie—or, what *is* your name?"

"Squatty," said the boy. Then noticing the look of surprise upon my face, he added soberly: "That ain't my 'sure-enough' name, you know; that's what the *boys* calls me. *Sis* calls me Jamesy."

"Well, Jamesy," I continued, buttoning my collar and drawing on my gloves, "I'm mighty glad to see you, and if you don't believe it, just go down in that right-hand overcoat-pocket and you'll find out."

The little fellow needed no second invitation, and as he drew forth a closely folded package the look of curiosity upon his face deepened to one of blank bewilderment.

"Open it," said I, smiling at the puzzled little face; "open it—it's for you."

"Oh, here, Cap," said the boy, dropping the package on the seat, and holding up a rigid finger, "you're a-givin' me this, ain't you?"

"I'm giving you the package, certainly," said I, somewhat bewildered. "Open it—it's a Christmas present for you—open it."

"What's your idy o' layin' fer me?" asked the boy, with a troubled and uneasy air. "I've been a-givin' you square business right along, ain't I?"

"Why, Jamesy," said I, as I vaguely comprehended the real drift of his thought, "the package *is* for you, and if you won't open it I will," and as I spoke I began unfolding it. "Here," said I, "is a pair of gloves, a little girl, about your size, told me to give to you, because I was telling her about you, over where I live, and it's 'a clear case,'" and I laughed lightly to myself as I noticed a slow flush creeping to his face. "And here," said I,

JAMESY

"is a 'bang up' pair of good old-fashioned socks, and, if they'll fit you, there's an old woman that wears specs and a mole on her nose, told me to tell you, for her, that she knit them for your Christmas present, and if you don't wear them she'll never forgive you. And here," I continued, "is a cap, as fuzzy as a woolly-worm, and as warm a cap, I reckon, as you ever stood on your head in; it's a cheap cap, but I bought it with my own money, and money that I worked mighty hard to get, because I ain't rich; now, if I was rich, I'd buy you a plug; but I've got an idea that this little, old, woolly cap, with earbobs to it, and a snapper to go under your chin, don't you see, won't be a bad cap to knock around in, such weather as this. What do you say now! Try her on once," and as I spoke I turned to place it on his head.

"Oomh-ooh!" he negatively murmured, putting out his hand, his closed lips quivering—the little frowzy head drooping forward, and the ragged shoes shuffling on the floor.

"Come," said I, my own voice growing curiously changed; "won't you take these presents? They are yours; you must accept them, Jamesy, not because they're worth so very much, or because they're very fine," I continued, bending down and folding up the parcel, "but because, you know, I want you to, and—

and—you must take them; you must!" and as I concluded, I thrust the tightly folded parcel beneath his arm, and pressed the little tattered elbow firmly over it.

"There you are," said I.—"Freeze onto it, and we'll skip off here at the avenue. Come."

I hardly dared to look behind me till I found myself upon the street, but as I threw an eager glance over my shoulder I saw the little fellow following, not bounding joyfully, but with a solemn step, the little parcel hugged closely to his side, and his eyes bent soberly upon the frozen ground.

"And how's Sis by this time?" I asked cheerily, flinging the question backward, and walking on more briskly.

"'Bout the same," said the boy, brightening a little, and skipping into a livelier pace.

"About the same, eh? and how's that?" I asked.

"Oh, she can't git around much like she used to, you know; but she's a-gittin' better all the time. She set up mighty nigh all day yisterday"; and as the boy spoke the eyes lifted with the old flash, and the little frowzy head tossed with the old defiance.

"Why, she's not down sick?" said I, a sudden ache of sorrow smiting me.

"Yes," replied the boy, "she's been bad a long time. You see," he broke in by way of explanation, "she didn't

JAMESY

have no shoes ner nothin' when winter come, and kindo' took cold, you know, and that give her the whoopin'-cough so's she couldn't git around much. You jist ort to see her now!—Oh, she's a-gittin' all right *now*, you can bet! and she said yesterday she'd be plum well Christmas, and that's on'y to-morry.—*Guess not!*" and as the little fellow concluded this exultant speech, he circled round me, and then shot forward like a rocket.

"Hi! Jamesy!" I called after him, pausing at a stairway and stepping in the door.

The little fellow joined me in an instant. "Want that shine now?" he inquired with panting eagerness.

"Not now, Jamesy," said I, "for I'm going to be quite busy for a while. This is my stopping-place here—the second door on the right, up-stairs, remember—and I work there when I'm in the city, and I sometimes sleep there, when I work late. And now I want to ask a very special favor of you," I continued, taking a little sealed packet from my vest: "here's a little box that you're to take to Sis, with my compliments—the compliments of the season, you understand,—and tell her I sent it, with particular directions that she shouldn't break it open till Christmas morning—not till Christmas morning, understand! Then you tell her that I would like very much to come and see her, and if she says all right,—and you must give me a good 'send-off,' and she'll say all right if 'Jamesy' says all right,—then come back here, say two hours from now, or three hours, or to-night anyway, and we'll go down and see Sis together—what do you say?"

The boy nodded dubiously. "Honest—must I do all that, sure enough?"

"Will you?" said I; "that's what I want to know"; and I pushed back the dusky little face and looked into the bewildered eyes.

"*Solid?*" he queried, gravely.

"'Solid,'" I repeated, handing him the box. "Will you come?"

"W'y, 'course I will, on'y I was jist a-thinkin'—"

"Just thinking what?" said I, as the little fellow paused abruptly and shook the box suspiciously at his ear. "Just thinking what?" I repeated; "for I must go now; good-bye.—Just thinking what?"

"Oh, nothin'," said the boy, backing off and staring at me in a phase of wonder akin to awe.—"Nothin', on'y I was jist a-thinkin' that you was a little the curiousest rooster *I* ever see."

Three hours later, as I sat alone, he came in upon me timidly to say he had not been home yet, having "run acrost the old man jist a-bilin', and had to git him corralled 'fore he dropped down somers in the snow;

JAMESY

but I'm a-gittin' 'long bully with him *now*," he added with a deep sigh of relief, "'cause he's so full he'll haf to let go purty soon. Say you'll be here?"

I nodded silently, and he was gone.

The merry peals of laughter rang up from the streets like mockery. The jingling of bells, the clatter and confusion of the swarming thoroughfares, flung up to me not one glad murmur of delight; the faint and far-off blaring of a dreamy waltz, blown breeze-like over the drowsy ear of night, had sounded sweeter to me had I stood amidst the band, with every bellowing horn about my ears, and the drums and clashing cymbals howling mad.

I couldn't work, I couldn't read, I couldn't rest; I could only pace about. I heard the clock strike ten, and strike it hard; I heard it strike eleven, viciously; and twelve it held out at arm's-length, and struck it full between the eyes, and let it drop—stone dead. O I saw the blood ooze from its ears, and saw the white foam freeze upon its lips! I was alone—alone!

It was three o'clock before the boy returned.

"Been a long while," he began, "but I had a fearful time with the old man, and he went on so when I *did* git him in I was 'most afeard to leave him; but he kindo' went to sleep at last, and Molly *she* come over to see how Sis was a-gittin'; and Sis said she'd like to see *you* if you'd come *now*, you know, while they ain't no racket goin' on."

"Come, then," said I, buttoning my coat closely at the throat, "I am ready"; and a moment later we had stepped into the frosty night. We moved along in silence, the little fellow half running, half sliding along the frozen pavement in the lead; and I noted, with a pleasurable thrill, that he had donned the little fuzzy cap and mittens, and from time to time was flinging, as he ran, admiring glances at his shadow on the snow.

Our way veered but a little from the very centre of the city, but led mainly along through narrow streets and alley-ways, where the rear ends of massive business blocks had dwindled down to insignificant proportions to leer grimly at us as we passed little grated windows and low, scowling doors. Occasionally we passed a clump of empty boxes, barrels, and such debris of merchandise as had been crowded pell-mell from some inner storage by their newer and more dignified companions; and now and then we passed an empty bus, bulging up in the darkness like a behemoth of the olden times; or, jutting from still narrower passages, the sloping ends of drays and carts innumerable. And along even as forbidding a defile as this we groped until we came upon a low, square brick building that might have served at one time as a wash-house, or, less probably, perhaps, a dairy. There was but one window in the front, and that but little larger than an ordinary pane of glass. In the sides, however, and higher up, was a row of gratings, evidently designed more to serve as ventilation than as openings for light. There was but one opening, an upright doorway, half above ground, half below, with little narrow side-steps leading down to it. A light shone dimly from the little window, and as the boy motioned me to pause and listen, a sound of female voices talking in an undertone was audible, mingled with a sound like that of some one snoring heavily.

"Hear the old man a-gittin' in his work?" whispered the boy.

I nodded. "He's asleep?"

"You *bet* he's asleep!" said the boy, still in a whisper; "and he'll jist about stay with it thataway fer five hours, anyhow. What time you got now, Cap?"

"A quarter now till four," I replied, peering at my watch.

"W'y, it's *Christmas*, then!" he cried in muffled rapture of delight; but abruptly checking his emotion, he beckoned me a little farther from the door, and spoke in a confidential whisper.

"Cap, look here, now; 'fore we go in I want you to promise me one thing—'cause you can fix it and *she'll* never drop! Now, here, I want to put up a job on Sis, you understand!"

"What!" I exclaimed, starting back and staring at the boy in amazement. "Put up a job on Sis?"

"Oh, look here, now, Cap; you ain't a-goin' back on a feller like that!" broke in the little fellow, in a mingled tone of pleading and reproof; "and if you don't help a feller I'll haf to wait till broad daylight, 'cause we ain't got no clock."

"No clock!" I repeated with increased bewilderment.

"Oh, come, Cap, what do you say? It ain't no lie, you know; all you got to do'll be to jist tell Sis it's Christmas—as though you didn't want *me* to hear, you know; and then she'll git my 'Christmas Gift!' *first*, you know;—and, oh, lordy! won't she think she's played it fine!" And as I slowly comprehended the meaning of the little fellow's plot I nodded my willingness to assist in "putting up the job."

"Now, hold on a second!" continued the little fellow, in the wildest glee, darting through an opening in a high board-fence a dozen steps away, and in an instant reappearing with a bulky parcel, which, as he neared me, I discovered was a paper flour-sack half filled, the other half lapped down and fastened with a large twine string. "Now this stuff," he went on excitedly, "you must juggle in without Sis seein' it—here, shove it under your 'ben,' here—there—that's business! Now when you go in, you're to set down with the other side to'rds the bed, you see, and when Sis *hollers* '*Christmas Gift*,' you know, you jist kindo' let it slide down to the floor like, and I'll nail it slick enough—though I'll p'tend, you know, it *ain't* Christmas yet, and look sold out, and say it wasn't fair fer you to tell her, and all that; and then I'll open up suddent-like, and if you don't see old Sis bug out them eyes of hern I don't want a cent!" And as the gleeful boy concluded this speech, he put his hands over his mouth and dragged me down the little, narrow steps.

"Here's that feller come to see you, Sis!" he announced abruptly, opening the door and peering in. "Come on," he said, turning to me. I followed, closing the door, and looking curiously around. A squabby, red-faced woman, sitting on the edge of a low bed, leered upon me, but with no salutation. An old cookstove, propped up with bricks, stood back against the wall directly opposite, and through the warped and broken doors in front sent out a dismal suggestion of the fire that burned within. At the side of this, prone upon the floor, lay the wretched figure of a man, evidently in the deepest stage of drunkenness, and thrown loosely over him was an old tattered piece of carpet and a little checkered shawl.

There was no furniture to speak of; one chair—and that was serving as a stand—sat near the bed, a high humpshouldered bottle sitting on it, a fruit-can full of water, and a little dim and smoky lamp that glared sulkily.

"Jamesy, can't you git the man a cheer er somepin'?" queried a thin voice from the bed; at which the red-faced woman rose reluctantly with the rather sullen words: "He can sit here, I reckon," while the boy looked at me significantly and took up a position near the "stand."

"So this is Sis?" I said, with reverence.

The little, haggard face I bent above was beautiful. The eyes were dark and tender—very tender, and though deeply sunken were most childish in expression and star-pure and luminous. She reached a wasted little hand out to me, saying simply: "It was mighty good in you to give them things to Jamesy, and send me that mo—that —that little box, you know—on'y I guess I—I won't need it." As she spoke a smile of perfect sweetness rested on the face, and the hand within my own nestled in dove-like peace.

JAMESY

The boy bent over the white face from behind and whispered something in her ear, trailing the little laughing lips across her brow as he looked up.

"Not now, Jamesy; wait awhile."

"Ah!" said I, shaking my head with feigned merriment, "don't you two go to plotting about me!"

"Oh, hello, no, Cap?" exclaimed the boy, assuringly. "I was on'y jist a-tellin' Sis to ast you if she mightn't open that box *now*—honest! And you jist ask her if you don't believe me—*I* won't listen." And the little fellow gave me a look of the most penetrative suggestiveness; and when a moment later the glad words, "Christmas Gift! Jamesy," rang out quaveringly in the thin voice, the little fellow snatched the sack up, in a paroxysm of delight, and before the girl had time to lift the long dark lashes once upon his merry face, he had emptied its contents out tumultuously upon the bed.

"You got it onto me, Sis!" cried the little fellow, dancing wildly round the room; "got it onto me *this* time! but I'm *game*, don't you fergit, and don't put up nothin' snide! How'll them shoes there ketch you? and how's this fer a cloak?—is them enough beads to suit you? And how's this fer a hat—feather and all? And how's this fer a dress—made and ever'thing? and I'd a-got a *corsik* with it if he'd a on'y had any little enough. *You* won't look fly ner nothin' when you throw all that style on you in the morning!—*Guess not!*" And the delighted boy went off upon another wild excursion round the room.

"Lean down here," said the girl, a great light in her eyes and the other slender hand sliding from beneath the covering. "Here is the box you sent me, and I've *opened* it—it wasn't *right*, you know, but somepin' kindo' said to open it *'fore* morning—and—and I opened it." And the eyes seemed asking my forgiveness, yet filled with great bewilderment. "You see," she went on, the thin voice falling in a fainter tone, "I *knowed* that money in the box—that is, the *bills*—I knowed them bills, 'cause *one* of 'em had a ink-spot on it, and the other ones had been pinned with it—they *wasn't* pinned together when *you* sent 'em, but the holes was in where they *had been* pinned, and they was all pinned together when *Jamesy* had 'em—'cause Jamesy used to have them very bills—he didn't think *I* knowed,—but onc't when he was asleep, and *father* was a-goin' through his clothes, I happened to find 'em in his coat 'fore *he* did; and I *counted* 'em, and hid 'em back ag'in, and father didn't find 'em, and Jamesy never knowed it.—I never said nothin', 'cause somepin' kindo' said to me it was all right; and somepin' kindo' said I'd git all these things here, too

JAMESY

—on'y I won't need 'em, ner the money, nor nothin'. How did *you* get the money? That's all!"

The boy had by this time approached the bed, and was gazing curiously upon the solemn little face.

"What's the *matter* with you, Sis?" he asked in wonderment; "ain't you glad?"

"I'm *mighty* glad, Jamesy," she said, the little, thin hands reaching for his own. "Guess I'm *too* glad, 'cause I can't do nothin' on'y jist *feel* glad; and somepin' kindo' says that that's the gladdest glad in all the world. Jamesy!"

"Oh, shaw, Sis! Why don't you tell a feller what's the matter?" said the boy, uneasily.

The white hands linked more closely with the brown, and the pure face lifted to the grimy one till they were blent together in a kiss.

"Be good to father, fer you know he used to be so good to us."

"O Sis! Sis!"

"Molly!"

The squabby, red-faced woman threw herself upon her knees and kissed the thin hands wildly and with sobs.

"Molly, somepin' kindo' says that *you* must dress me in the morning—but I won't need the hat, and you must

JAMESY

take it home fer Nannie— Don't—don't cry so loud; you'll wake father."

I bent my head down above the frowzy one and moaned—moaned.

"And you, sir," went on the failing voice, reaching for my hand, "you—you must take this money back—you must take it back, fer I don't need it. You must take it back and—and—give it—give it to the poor." And even with the utterance upon the gracious lips the glad soul leaped and fluttered through the open gates.

AN ADJUSTABLE LUNATIC

AN ADJUSTABLE LUNATIC

"An 'adjustable lunatic'?"

"Yes, sir, an adjustable lunatic—you may know I don't make a business of insanity, or I wouldn't be running at large here on the streets of the city."

It was on the morning of St. Patrick's Day. I had been drifting aimlessly around the city for hours, tossed about by the restless tide of humanity that ebbed and flowed in true sea-fashion at the Washington and Illinois street crossing. The few friends I had been fortunate enough to fall in with prior to the parade I had been unfortunate enough to lose in the flurry and excitement attending that event; and, brought to a sudden anchorage at the Bates House landing, I found myself at the mercy of a boundless throng that held not one familiar face. It was a literal jam at that juncture, and anxious and impatient as I was to break away, I was forced into a bondage which, though not exactly agreeable, was at least the source of an experience that will linger in my memory fresh and clear when every other feature of the day shall have faded.

I had been crowded into a position on a step of the stairway that gave me a lean upon the balustrade and placed me head and shoulders above the crowd; and although I comprehended the helplessness of my position, I was, in a manner, thankful for the opportunity it afforded me to study the unsuspecting subjects just below. As my hungry eyes went foraging about from face to face they fell upon the features of an individual so singularly abstracted in appearance and so apparently oblivious to his surroundings, that I mentally congratulated him upon his enviable disposition.

He was a slender man, of thirty years, perhaps; not tall, but something over medium height; he had dark hair and eyes, with a complexion much too fair to correspond; was not richly dressed, but neatly, and in good taste.

Instinctively I wondered who and what he was; and my speculative fancy went to work and made a lawyer of him—then a minister—an artist—a musician—an actor—and a dancing-master. Suddenly I found my stare returned with equal fervor, and tried to look away, but something held me. He was elbowing his way to where I stood, and smiling as he came.

AN ADJUSTABLE LUNATIC

"I don't know you," he said, when, after an almost superhuman effort, he had gained my side, to the discomfiture of a brace of mangy little bootblacks that occupied the step below—"I don't know you personally, but you look bored. I'm troubled with the same disease and want company—as the poet of the Sierras wails, 'How all alone a man may be in crowds!'" Something in the utterance made me offer him my hand.

He grasped it warmly. "It's curious," he said, "how friends are made and where true fellowship begins. Now we've known each other all our lives and never met before. What d'ye say?"

I smiled approval at the odd assertion.

"But tell me," he continued, "what conclusion you have arrived at in your study of me; come, now, be frank —what do you make of me?"

Although I found myself considerably startled, I feigned composure and acknowledged that I had been speculating as to who and what he was, but found myself unable to define a special character.

"I thought so," he said. "No one ever reads my character—no one ever will. Why, I've had phrenologists groping around among my bumps by the hour to no purpose, and physiognomists driving themselves crosseyed; but they never found it, and they never will. The

AN ADJUSTABLE LUNATIC

very things of which I am capable they invariably place beyond my capacity; and, with like sageness, the very things I can't do they declare me to be a master hand at. But I like to worry them; it's fun for me. Why, old Fowler himself, here the other night, thumbed my head as mellow as a May-apple, and never came within a mile of it! Some characters are readable enough, I'm willing to admit. Your face, for instance, is a bulletin-board to me, but you can't read mine, for I'm neither a doctor, lawyer, artist, actor, musician, nor anything else you may have in your mind. You might guess your way all through the dictionary and then not get it. It's simply an impossibility, that's all."

I laughed uneasily, for although amused at the quaint humor of his language, a nervous fluttering of the eyes and a spasmodic twitching of the corners of his mouth made me think his manner merely an affectation. But I was interested, and as his conversation seemed to invite the interrogation, I flatly asked him to indulge my curiosity and tell me what he was.

"Wait till the crowd thins, and maybe I will. In the meantime here's a cigar and here's a light—as Mr. Quilp playfully remarks to Tom Scott—'Smoke away, you dog you!'"

"Well, you're a character," said I, dubiously.

AN ADJUSTABLE LUNATIC

"Yes," he replied, "but you can't tell what kind, and I can tell you the very trade you work at."

I smiled incredulously.

"Now don't look lofty and assume a professional air, for you're only a mechanic, and a sign-painter at that."

Although he spoke with little courtesy of address, there was a subtle something in his eye that drew me magnet-like and held me. I was silent.

"Want to know how I became aware of that fact?" he went on, with a quick, sharp glance at my bewildered face. "There's nothing wonderful about my knowing that; I've had my eye on you for two hours, and you stare at every sign-board you pass, worse than a country-jake; and once or twice I saw you stop and study carefully some fresh design, or some new style of letter. You're a stranger here in the city, too. Want to know how I can tell? Because you walk like you were actually going some place; but I notice that you never get there, for continually crossing and recrossing streets, and backtracking past show-windows, and congratulating yourself, doubtless, upon the thorough business air of your reflection in the plate glass. Come, we can get through now; let's walk."

I followed him unhesitatingly. To say that I was

AN ADJUSTABLE LUNATIC

simply curious would be too mild; I was fascinated, and to that degree I actually fastened on his arm, and clung there till we had quite escaped the crowd. "I like you, some way," he said, "but you're too impulsive; you let your fancy get away with your better judgment. Now, you don't know me, and I'm even pondering whether to frankly unbosom to you, or give you the slip; and I'll not leave the proposition to you to decide, for I know you'd say 'unbosom'; so I'll think about it quietly for a while yet and give you an unbiassed verdict."

We walked on in silence for the distance, perhaps, of half a dozen blocks, turning and angling about till we came upon an open stairway in an old unpainted brick building, where my strange companion seemed to pause mechanically.

"Do you live here?" I asked.

"I stay here," he replied, "for I don't call it living to be fastened up in this old sepulchre. I like it well enough at night, for then I feast and fatten on the gloom and glower that infest it; but in the normal atmosphere of day my own room looks repellant, and I only visit it, as now, out of sheer desperation."

If I had at first been mystified with this curious being, I was by this time thoroughly bewildered. The more I studied him the more at a loss I was to fathom him; and

AN ADJUSTABLE LUNATIC

as I stood staring blankly in his face, he exclaimed almost derisively: "You give it up, don't you?"

I nodded.

"Well," he continued, "that's a good sign, and I've concluded to 'unbosom':—I'm an adjustable lunatic."

"An 'adjustable lunatic'!" I repeated, blankly. And after the remarkable proposition that ushers in the story, he continued smilingly:

"Don't be alarmed, now, for I'm glad to assure you of the fact that I'm as harmless as a baby-butterfly. Nobody knows I'm crazy, nobody ever dreams of such a thing—and why?—Because the faculty is adjustable, don't you see, and self-controlling. I never allow it to interfere with business matters, and only let it on at leisure intervals for the amusement it affords me in the pleasurable break it makes in the monotony of a matter-of-fact existence. I'm off duty to-day—in fact, I've been off duty for a week; or, to be franker still, I lost my situation ten days ago, and I've been humoring this propensity in the meanwhile; and now, if you're inclined to go up to my room with me—the windows are both raised, you see, and you can call for help should occasion require; people are constantly passing—if you feel inclined, I say, to go up with me, I'll do my best to entertain you. I like you, as I said before, and you can trust me, I assure you. Come."

If I were to attempt a description of the feelings that possessed me as I followed my strange acquaintance up the stairway, I should fail as utterly as one who would attempt to portray the experience of lying in a nine-days' trance, so I leave the reader's fancy to befriend me, and hasten on to more tangible matters.

We paused at the first landing, my companion unlocking a door on the right, and handing me the key with the remark: "You may feel safer with it. And don't be frightened," he continued, "when I open the door, for it always whines like somebody had stepped on its knob," and I laughed at the odd figure as he threw the door open and motioned me to enter.

It was a queer apartment, filled with a jumbled array of old chairs and stands; old trunks, a lounge, and a stack of odd-shaped packages. A frowzy carpet thrown over the floor like a blanket, and a candle-box spittoon with a broken lamp-chimney in it. A little swinging shelf of dusty books, with a railroad map pasted just above it. A narrow table with a telegraph instrument attached, and wires like ivy-vines running all about the walls; and scattered around the instrument was an endless array of zinc and copper scraps, and bits of brass, spiral springs, and queer-shaped little tools. A flute propped up one window, and near it, on another stand, a cornet and an old guitar; a pencil sketch half finished, and a stuffed glove with a pencil in its fingers lying on it; a spirit-lamp, a lump of beeswax, and a hundred other odds and ends, betokening the presence of some mechanical, musical, scientific genius.

"It's a bachelor's room," said the host, noting my inquisitive air.—"It's a bachelor's room, so you'll expect no apologies. Sit down when you're through with the industrial, and turn your attention to the art department."

I followed the direction of his hand, and my eyes fell upon a painted face of such ineffable sweetness and beauty I was fairly dazed. It was not an earthly form, at least in coloring, for the features seemed to glow with beatific light. The eyes were large, dark, and dewy, thrown upward with a longing look, and filled with such intensity of tenderness one could but sigh to see them. The hair, swept negligently back, fell down the gleaming shoulders like a silken robe, and nestled in its glossy waves the ears peeped shyly out like lily-blooms. The lips were parted with an utterance that one could almost hear, and weep because the blessed voice was mute. The hands were folded on a crumpled letter and pressed close against the heart, and a curl of golden hair was coiled around the fingers.

"Is it a creation of the fancy?" I asked.

"Well, yes," he answered, with a dreamy drawl. "I call it fancy, when in a normal state; but now," he continued, in a fainter tone, "I will designate it as a portrait." And oh, so sad, so hopeless and despairing was the utterance, it seemed to well up from the fountain of his heart like a spray of purest sorrow.

"Who painted it?" I asked.

"'Who painted it?'" he repeated, drowsily—"'who painted it?' Oh, no; I mustn't tell you that; for if I answered you with 'Raphael,' you'd say, 'Ah, no! the paint's too fresh for that, and he's been dead for ages. 'Who painted it?' No, no, I mustn't tell you that!"

"But are you not an artist?—I see an easel in the corner there, and here's a maulstick lying on the mantel."

"I an artist? Why, man, what ails you? I told you not ten minutes since that I was an adjustable lunatic; and don't you see I am?—You can't mislead me nor throw me off my guard. When it comes to reason or solid logic, don't you find me there? And here again, to show the clearness of my judgment, I remove the cause of our little dissension, and our friendly equanimity is restored—" and he turned the picture to the wall.

AN ADJUSTABLE LUNATIC

I could but smile at the gravity and adroitness of his language and demeanor.

"There," said he, smiling in return; "your face is brighter than the day outside; let's change the topic. Do you like music?"

"Passionately," I responded. "Will you play?"

"No; I will sing."

He took the guitar from the table, and, with a prelude wilder than the "Witches' Dance," he sang a song he called "The Dream of Death," a grievously sad song, so full of minor tones and wailing words, the burden of it still lingers in my ears:

> "O gentle death, bow down and sip
> The soul that lingers on my lip;
> O gentle death, bow down and keep
> Eternal vigil o'er my sleep;
> For I am weary and would rest
> Forever on your loving breast."

His voice, as plaintive as a dove's, went trailing through the rondel like weariness itself; and when at last it died away in one long quaver of ecstatic melody, though I felt within my heart an echoing of grief

> "Too sweetly sad to name as pain,"

I broke the silence following to remind him of his having told me he was not a musician.

"Only a novice," he responded.—"One may twang a lute and yet not be a troubadour. By the way," he broke off abruptly, "is that expression original with me, or have I picked it up in some old book of rhyme?—Oh, yes! How do you like poetry?"

He sprang to his feet as he spoke, and without awaiting an answer to his query went diving about in a huge waste-basket standing near the table.

"It's a thing I dislike to acknowledge," he went on, "but I don't mind telling you. The fact is, I'm a follower of Wegg and sometimes 'drop into poetry—as a friend,' you understand; and if you'll 'lend me your ears,' I'll give you a specimen of my versification."

He had drawn up a roll of paper from the debris of the basket, and unrolling it with a flourish, and a mock-heroic air of inspiration, he read as follows:

> "A fantasy that came to me
>   As wild and wantonly designed
> As ever any dream might be
>   Unraveled from a madman's mind,—
> A tangle-work of tissue, wrought
>   By cunning of the spider-brain,
>   And woven, in an hour of pain,
> To trap the giddy flies of thought——."

AN ADJUSTABLE LUNATIC

He paused, and with a look of almost wild entreaty he pleaded: "You understand it, don't you?"

I nodded hesitatingly.

"Why, certainly you do. The meaning's the plainest thing in it. What's your idea of its meaning? tell me! —Why don't you tell me!"

"Read it again that I may note it carefully."

He repeated it.

"Why," said I, "it appears to me to be the introduction to a poem written under peculiar circumstances, and containing, perhaps, some strange ideas that the author would excuse for the reason of their coming in the way they did."

"Right!" he exclaimed, joyously; "and now if you'll give me your most critical attention, and promise not to interrupt, I'll read the poem entire."

"Go on," I said, for I was far more eager to listen than I would have him know.

"And will you excuse any little wildness of gesture or expression that I may see fit to introduce in the rendition?"

"Certainly," said I, "certainly; go on!"

"And you won't interrupt or get excited? Light another cigar; and here's a chair to throw your feet across. Now, unbutton your coat and lean back. Are you thoroughly comfortable?"

AN ADJUSTABLE LUNATIC

"Thoroughly," said I, impatiently—"a thousand thoroughlies."

"All right," he said; "I'm glad to hear you say it; but before I proceed I desire to call your attention to the fact that this poem is a literary orphan—a foundling, you understand?"

"I understand; go on."

And with a manner all too wild to be described, he read, or rather recited, the following monstrosity of rhyme:

> "I stood beneath a summer moon
>   All swollen to uncanny girth,
> And hanging, like the sun at noon,
>   Above the centre of the earth;
>   But with a sad and sallow light,
>   As it had sickened of the night
> And fallen in a pallid swoon.
> Around me I could hear the rush
>   Of sullen winds, and feel the whirr
> Of unseen wings apast me brush
>   Like phantoms round a sepulchre;
> And, like a carpeting of plush,
>   A lawn unrolled beneath my feet,
>   Bespangled o'er with flowers as sweet
>   To look upon as those that nod
>   Within the garden-fields of God,

AN ADJUSTABLE LUNATIC

But odorless as those that blow
In ashes in the shades below.

"And on my hearing fell a storm
    Of gusty music, sadder yet
    Than every whimper of regret
  That sobbing utterance could form,
    And patched with scraps of sound that seemed
    Torn out of tunes that demons dreamed,
    And pitched to such a piercing key,
    It stabbed the ear with agony;
    And when at last it lulled and died,
    I stood aghast and terrified.
  I shuddered and I shut my eyes,
    And still could see, and feel aware
    Some mystic presence waited there;
  And staring, with a dazed surprise,
    I saw a creature so divine
    That never subtle thought of mine
    May reproduce to inner sight
    So fair a vision of delight.

"A syllable of dew that drips
  From out a lily's laughing lips
  Could not be sweeter than the word
  I listened to, yet never heard.—
  For, oh, the woman hiding there

AN ADJUSTABLE LUNATIC

Within the shadows of her hair,
Spake to me in an undertone
So delicate, my soul alone
But understood it as a moan
Of some weak melody of wind
A heavenward breeze had left behind.

"A tracery of trees, grotesque
    Against the sky, behind her seen,
Like shapeless shapes of arabesque
    Wrought in an Oriental screen;
And tall, austere and statuesque
    She loomed before it—e'en as though
      The spirit-hand of Angelo
      Had chiselled her to life complete,
    With chips of moonshine round her feet.
And I grew jealous of the dusk,
    To see it softly touch her face,
    As lover-like, with fond embrace,
It folded round her like a husk:
But when the glitter of her hand,
    Like wasted glory, beckoned me,
    My eyes grew blurred and dull and dim—
    My vision failed—I could not see—
I could not stir—I could but stand,
    Till, quivering in every limb,
    I flung me prone, as though to swim

AN ADJUSTABLE LUNATIC

    The tide of grass whose waves of green
    Went rolling ocean-wide between
    My helpless shipwrecked heart and her
    Who claimed me for a worshipper.

"And writhing thus in my despair,
    I heard a weird, unearthly sound,
    That seemed to lift me from the ground
And hold me floating in the air.
I looked, and lo! I saw her bow
    Above a harp within her hands;
A crown of blossoms bound her brow,
    And on her harp were twisted strands
Of silken starlight, rippling o'er
With music never heard before
By mortal ears; and, at the strain,
I felt my Spirit snap its chain
And break away,—and I could see
It as it turned and fled from me
To greet its mistress, where she smiled
To see the phantom dancing wild
And wizard-like before the spell
Her mystic fingers knew so well."

I sat throughout it all as though under the strange influence of an Eastern drug. My fancy was so wrought upon I only saw the reader mistily, and clothed, as it were, in a bedragoned costume of the Orient. My mind seemed idle—steeped in drowse and languor, and yet peopled with a thousand shadowy fancies that came trooping from chaotic hiding-places, and mingling in a revelry of such riotous extravagance it seemed a holiday of elfish thought.

I shook my head, I rubbed my eyes, arose bewildered, and sat down again; arose again and walked across the room, my strange companion following every motion with an intensity of gaze almost mesmeric.

"You fail to comprehend it?" he queried.

I shook my head.

"You can almost grasp it, can't you?"

"Yes," I answered.

"But not quite?"

"Not quite."

"Does it worry you?"

"Yes."

"Think it will cling to you, and fret you, vex you, haunt you?"

"I know it will."

"Think you'll ever fully comprehend it?"

"I can't say," I replied, thoughtfully.—"Perhaps I may in time. Will you allow me to copy it?"

AN ADJUSTABLE LUNATIC

"What do you want with it?"

"I want to study it," I replied.

"And you're sure you don't understand it, and it worries you, and frets you, and vexes you, and haunts you? Good! I'll read you the final clause now; that may throw a light of some kind on it"; and, opening the scroll, again he read:

>"What is it? Who will rightly guess
> If it be ought but nothingness
> That dribbles from a wayward pen
> To spatter in the eyes of men?
> What matter! I will call it mine,
> And I will take the changeling home
> And bathe its face with morning-shine,
> And comb it with a golden comb
> Till every tangled tress of rhyme
> Will fairer be than summer-time:
> And I will nurse it on my knee,
> And dandle it beyond the clasp
> Of hands that grip and hands that grasp,
> Through life and all eternity!"

"Now what do you think of it?" he asked with a savageness that startled me.

"I am more at sea than ever," I replied.

"Well, I wish you a prosperous voyage! Here's the

poem; I've another copy. 'Read and reflect,' as the railroad poster says, but don't you publish it—at least while I'm alive, for I've no thirst for literary fame—I only write for home-use; but you're a good fellow, and I like you for all your weak points, and I trust the confidence I repose will not be disregarded. Come!"

He had opened the door and was holding out his hand for the key.

I gave it to him and followed out mechanically. He left the door ajar and followed to the bottom of the stairs.

"And now if you'll pardon me," he said, "I'll say good-bye to you here; I've some packing to do and ought to be at it."

"Why, you're not going to leave the city?" I asked.

"Well, no, not to-day; but the jig's up with me here, and it's only a question of time—I can't hold out much longer—as our rural friend remarks, 'Money matters is mighty sceerce'; and if I don't pull out shortly I'll have to 'fold my tent like the Bedouin and silently plagiarize away!'"

"If I could be of any assistance to you—" I began, but he checked me abruptly with, "Oh, no, I don't require it, I assure you; I've two dollars to your one, doubtless. Thank you just the same, and good-bye. Here's my card; it's not my name, however, but it'll answer; I'll not see you again, though you should live to be as bald as a brickyard, for, my dear young friend, I'm going away. Good-bye, and may all good things overtake you!"

He gripped my hand like a vice, and turning quickly, went skipping up the stairway two steps at a time.

"Good-bye!" I called to him, sorrowfully; then turned reluctantly away, examining the card he had given me, which, to my astonishment, was not his card at all, but a railroad ticket entitling the bearer to a ride from Danville, Illinois, to York, Pennsylvania; this fact I remember quite distinctly, as I read it over and over, revolving in my mind the impression that this was but another instance of his eccentricity, or perhaps a trick by which I might be victimized in some undreamed-of way. But upon second thought I concluded it to be simply a mistake, and so turned back and called him to the window above and explained.

He came down and begged my pardon for the trouble he had given me, took the ticket, thanked me, and said good-bye again.

"But," said I, "you haven't given me your real card in exchange."

"Oh, no matter!" he said smilingly. "Call me Smith,

Jones, or Robinson, it's all the same; good-bye, and don't forget your old friend and well-wisher, the Adjustable Lunatic." And even thus he vanished from my sight forever.

The remainder of the day and half of the night I spent in studious contemplation of the curious composition, but without arriving at any tangible conclusion. I am still engaged with my investigation. Sometimes the meaning seems almost within my mental grasp; but, balancing, adjusting, and comparing its many curious bearings, I find my judgment persistently at fault. It has puzzled and bewildered me for weeks. No line of it but canters through my brain like a fractious nightmare; no syllable but fastens on my fancy like a leech, and sucks away the life-blood of my every thought. I am troubled, worried, fretted, vexed, and haunted; and I write this now in the earnest hope that wiser minds may have an opportunity of making it a subject of investigation, and because one week ago to-day my eyes fell upon the following special telegram to the Indianapolis "Journal":

> PERU, IND., April 12.—An unknown man committed suicide in the eastward-bound train on the Wabash road, just below Waverly, at about 11 o'clock this morning. He had in his possession, besides the revolver with which he shot himself, a ticket

AN ADJUSTABLE LUNATIC

from Danville, Illinois, to York, Pennsylvania, a gold watch, $19 in money, a small valise, and some letters and other papers which indicated his name to be George S. Clofling.

He was shot twice in the region of the heart, and his revolver showed that between the first and last shots two cartridges missed fire.

TOD

TOD

STODDARD ANDERSON was the boy's name, though had you made inquiry for Stoddard Anderson of any boy of the town in which he lived—and I myself lived there, a handy boy in the dim old days—you doubtless would have been informed that nobody of that name was there. Your juvenile informant, however, by way of gratuitous intelligence, might have gone on to state that two families of the name of Anderson resided there,—"Old Do-good" Anderson, the preacher, and his brother John. But had you asked for "Tod" Anderson, or simply "Tod," your boy would have known Tod; your boy, in all likelihood, would have had especial reasons for remembering Tod, although his modesty, perhaps, might not allow him to inform you how Tod had "waxed it to him more'n onc't"! But he would have told you, as I tell you now, that Tod Anderson was the preacher's boy, and lived at the parsonage. Tod was a queer boy.

TOD

Stoddard Anderson was named in honor of some obscure divine his father had joined church under when a boy. It was a peculiar weakness of the father to relate the experience of his early conviction; and as he never tired of repeating it, by way of precept and admonition to the wayward lambkins of his flock, Tod mastered its most intricate and sacred phraseology, together even with the father's more religious formulas, to a degree of perfection that enabled him to preside at mock meetings in the hayloft, and offer the baptismal service at the "swimmin'-hole."

In point of personal or moral resemblance, Tod was in no wise like his father. Some said he was the picture of his mother, they who could remember her, for she fell asleep when Tod was three days old, with her mother-arms locked around him so closely that he cried, and they had to take him away from her. No.—Death had taken her away from him.

It needs now no chronicle to tell how Tod thrived in spite of his great loss, and how he grew to be a big, fat, two-fisted baby with a double chin, the pride and constant worry of the dear old grandmother into whose care he had fallen. It requires no space in history's crowded page to tell how he could stand up by a chair when eight months old, and crow and laugh and doddle his little chubby arms till he quite upset his balance, and, pulling the chair down with him, would laugh and crow louder than ever, and kick, and crawl, and sprawl, and jabber; and never lift a whimper of distress but when being rocked to sleep. Let a babyhood of usual interest be inferred—then add a few more years, and you will have the Tod of ten I knew.

O moral, saintlike, and consistent Christian, what is it in the souls of little children so antagonistic to your own sometimes? What is it in their wayward and impulsive natures that you cannot brook? And what strange tincture of rebellious feeling is it that embitters all the tenderness and love you pour out so lavishly upon their stubborn and resentful hearts? Why is it you so covetously cherish the command divine, "Children, obey your parents," and yet find no warm nook within the breast for that old houseless truth that goes wailing through the world:

"A boy's will is the wind's will,
And the thoughts of youth are long, long thoughts"?

Tod went to school—the thriftless Tod!—not wholly thriftless, either; for, although he had not that apt way of skimming like a swallow down the placid rills of learning, he did possess, in some mysterious strength, a most extraordinary knack of acquiring just such information as was not taught at school, and had no place within the busy hive of knowledge.

Tod was a failure in arithmetic. Tod couldn't tell twice ten from twice eternity. Tod knew absolutely nothing of either Christopher Columbus or the glorious country he discovered expressly for the use of industry and learning, as the teacher would have had him implicitly believe. Tod couldn't tell you anything of John Smith, even, that very noted captain who walks cheek by jowl with the dusky Pocahontas across the illimitable fancy of the ten-year-old school-boy of our glorious republic. Tod knew all about the famous Captain Kidd, however. In fact, Tod could sing his history with more lively interest and real appreciation than his fellow-schoolmates sang geography. The simple Tod once joined the geographical chorus with:

> "I'd a Bible in my hand,
> As I sailed, as I sailed,
> And I sunk her in the sand,
> As I sailed."

And Tod—not Captain Kidd—had a ringing in his ears as he sang, as he sang, and an overflow of tears as he sang. And then he ran away from school that afternoon, and sang Captain Kidd, from A to izzard, in the full hearing of the "Industrial Hive," to the very evident amusement of "the workers," and the discomfiture of the ruler of "the swarm."

The teacher called on the good minister that evening, and after a long talk on the back porch, left late in the dusk, wiping his eyes with one hand, and shaking the other very warmly with the preacher. And Tod slipped noiselessly along the roof above them, and slid down the other side, and watched the teacher's departure with a puzzled face.

Tod was at school next morning long before the call of "Books"; in fact, so early, that he availed himself of his isolated situation to chalk the handle of the teacher's pointer, to bore a gimlet-hole in the water-bucket, to slip a chip under one corner of the clock in order to tilt it out of balance and time, and in many more ingenious ways to contribute to the coming troubles of the day. The most audacious act, however, was to climb above the teacher's desk and paste a paper scrap over a letter "o" in the old motto, "Be good," that had offered him its vain advice for years. As one by one these depredations met the teacher's notice through the day, the culprit braced himself for some disastrous issue, but his only punishment was the assured glance the teacher always gave him, and the settled yet forbearing look of pain upon his face. In sheer daring Tod laughed aloud —a hollow, hungry laugh that had no mirth in it—but as suddenly subsided in a close investigation of a problem in mental arithmetic, when the teacher backed slowly toward his desk and stood covertly awaiting further developments. But he was left again to his own inclinations, after having, with a brazen air of innocence, solicited and gained the master's assistance in the solution of a very knotty problem, which it is needless to say he knew no more of than before. Throughout the remainder of the day Tod was thoughtful, and was evidently evolving in his mind a problem far more serious than could be found in books. Of his own accord, that evening at the close of school, he stayed in for some mysterious reason that even his own deskmate could not comprehend. When, an hour later, this latter worthy, from the old barn opposite, watched Tod and the teacher hand in hand come slowly down the walk, he whispered to himself with bated breath: "What's the durn fool up to, anyhow?"

From that time Tod grew to be a deeper mystery than he could fathom, inasmuch as some strange spirit of industry fell upon him, and he became a student.

Though a perverse fate had seemingly decreed that Tod should remain a failure in all branches wherein most

TOD

school-boys readily succeed, he rapidly advanced in reading; and in the declamatory art he soon acquired a fame that placed him high above the reach of competitors. Tod never cried when he got up to "speak." Tod never blanched, looked silly, and hung down his head. Tod never mumbled in an undertone, was never at a loss to use his hands, nor ever had "his piece" so poorly memorized that he must hesitate with awkward repetitions, to sit down at last in wordless misery among the unfeeling and derisive plaudits of the school. Tod, in a word, knew no such word as fail when his turn was called to entertain his hearers either with the gallant story of the youthful "Casabianca," "The Speech of Logan," or "Catiline's Defiance." Let a scholar be in training for the old-time exercises of Friday afternoon, and he was told to speak out clear and full—not hang his head—not let his arms hang down like empty sleeves,—but to stand up like a king, look everybody in the face, as though he were doing something to be proud of—in short, to take Tod for his model, and "speak out like a man"!

When Tod failed to make his appearance with his usual promptness one Friday afternoon, and the last day of the term, there was evidence of general disappointment. Tod was to deliver an oration written especially for that occasion by the teacher. The visitors were all there—the school committee, and the minister, Tod's father, who occupied Tod's desk alone when "Books" was called. The teacher, with his pallid, care-worn face, tiptoed up and down the aisles, bending occasionally to ask a whispered question, and to let the look of anxious wonder deepen on his face as the respectful pupils shook their heads in silent response. But upon a whispered colloquy with the minister, his face brightened, as he learned that "Tod was practising his oration in the wood-house half an hour before the ringing of the bell."

A boy was sent to bring him, but returned alone, to say that he had not been able to find any trace of him.

"Oh, he'll be here in time enough," said the teacher apologetically to the sad-faced minister.—"He's deeply interested in his effort for this afternoon, and I'm certain he wouldn't purposely disappoint me." The good man in reply shook his head resignedly, with a prayerful flight of the eyes indicative of long-suffering and forbearance.

The opening services of singing and prayer. No Tod.

First class in arithmetic called—examined. No Tod.

Second class, ditto; still no Tod. Primary class in ditto, composed of little twin sisters, aged six, with very red hair and very fair skin, and very short dresses and very slim legs. Tod failed to join his class.

TOD

The long-suffering minister was ill at ease. The exercise failed in some way to appease the hunger of the soul within. He looked out of the open window nervously, and watched a saucy little sapsucker hopping up and down a tree; first up one side and then down the other, suddenly disappearing near the roots, and as suddenly surprising him with a mischievous pecking near the top fork. He thought of his poor, wayward boy, with a vague, vague hope that he might yet, in some wise ruling of a gracious Providence, escape the gallows, and with a deep sigh turned to the noisy quiet of the school-room; he did not even smile as he took up Tod's geography, opened at the boy's latest work,—a picture of the State seal, where a stalwart pioneer in his shirt-sleeves hacked away at a gnarled and stubborn-looking tree, without deigning to notice a stampeding herd of buffalo that dashed by in most alarming proximity. The nonchalance of the sturdy yeoman was intensified by Tod's graphic pen, which had mounted each plunging monster with a daring rider, holding a slack bridle-rein in one hand, and with the other swinging a plug-hat in the most exultant and defiant manner. This piece of grotesque art and others equally suggestive of the outcropping genius of their author, were put wearily aside, only serving, as it seemed, to deepen rather than dissolve the gloom enshrouding the good father's face. And so the exercises wore along till recess came, and with it came the missing Tod.

"I'm in time, am I? Goody!" shouted Tod, jumping over a small boy who had stooped to pick up a slate-pencil, and stopping abruptly in front of the teacher's desk.

"Why, Tod; what in the world!"

Tod's features wore a proud, exultant smile, though somewhat glamoured with a network of spiteful-looking scratches; and his eyes were more than usually bright, although their lids were blue, and swollen to a size that half concealed them. His head, held jauntily erect, suggested nothing but boyish spirit; but his hair, tousled beyond all reason, with little wisps of it glued together with clots of blood; his best clothes soiled and torn; a bruised and naked knee showing through a straight rent across one leg of his trousers, conveyed the idea of a recent passage through some gantlet of disastrous fortune.

It was nothing, Tod said, only on his way to school he had come upon a blind man who played the fiddle and sold lead-pencils, and the boy who had been leading him had stolen something from him; and Tod had voluntarily started in pursuit of the fugitive, only to overtake him after a prolonged chase of more than a mile. "And now I've got you out o' town," said the offender, wheeling suddenly upon him, "I'll jist meller your head fer you!" After a long pause, in which Tod's face was hidden from the curious group about him, as the teacher bent above him at the back steps pouring water on his head, he continued: "Didn't think the little cuss was so stout! Oh! I'm scratched up, but you ought to see him! And you ought to hear him holler ' 'Nuff!' and you ought to see him hand over three boxes of pens and them penholders and pencils he stol'd, and a whole bunch o' envelopes; there's blood on some of 'em, and the blind man said I could keep 'em, and he give me a lead-pencil, too, with red in one end and blue in the other. Father, you sharpen it."

Tod never spoke better in his life than on that memorable afternoon—so well indeed did he acquit himself that the good old father failed to censure him that evening for the sin of fighting, and perhaps never would have done so had not the poor blind man so far forgotten the dignity of his great affliction as to get as drunk as he was blind two evenings following, and play the fiddle in front of the meeting-house during divine service.

It was in the vacation following these latter-mentioned incidents that an occurrence of far more seriousness took place.

TOD

Tod had never seen a circus, for until this eventful epoch in our simple history the humble little village had never been honored with the presence of this "most highly moral and instructive exhibition of the age." When the grand cavalcade, with its blaring music and its richly caparisoned horses, with their nodding plumes and spangles, four abreast, drawing the identical "fiery chariot" Tod had heard his father talk about; when all the highly painted wagons with their mysterious contents, and the cunning fairy ponies with their little, fluffy manes and flossy tails—when all this burst upon Tod's enraptured eyes, he fell mutely into place behind the band-wagon, with its myriad followers; and so, dazed, awe-stricken and entranced, accompanied the pageant on its grand triumphal march around the town.

Tod carried water for the animals; Tod ran errands of all kinds for the showmen; Tod looked upon the gruff, ill-tempered canvas-hand with an awe approaching reverence. Tod was going to the show, too, for he had been most fortunate in exchanging his poor services of the morning for the "open sesame" of all the dreamed-of wonders of the arena. Tod would laugh and whisper to himself, hugging the ticket closely to his palpitating side, as he ran about on errands of a hundred kinds, occupying every golden interlude of time in drawing the magic passport from his pocket and gloating over the cabalistic legend "Complimentary," with the accompanying autograph of the fat old manager with the broad, bejewelled expanse of shirt-front, and a watch-seal as big as a walnut; while on the reverse side he would glut his vision with an "exterior view of the monster pavilion," where a "girl poised high in air on a cord, in spangled dress," was kissing her hand to a mighty concourse of people, who waved their hats and handkerchiefs in wildest token of approval and acclaim. Nor was this the sole cause of Tod's delight, for the fat man with the big watch-seal had seemed to take a special fancy to him, and had told him he might bring a friend along, that his ticket would pass two. As the gleeful Tod was scampering off to ask the teacher if he wouldn't go, he met his anxious father in a deep state of distress, and was led home to listen in agony and tears to a dismal dissertation on the wickedness of shows, and the unending punishment awaiting the poor, giddy moths that fluttered round them. Tod was missed next morning. He had retired very early the evening previous. "He acted strange-like," said the good grandmother, recalling vaguely that he hadn't eaten any supper, "and I thought I heard him crying in the night. What was the matter with him, Isaac?"

Two weeks later Tod was discovered by his distracted father and an officer, cowering behind a roll of canvas, whereon a fat man sat declaring with a breezy nonchalance that no boy of Tod's description was "along o' this-'ere party." And the defiant Tod, when brought to light, emphatically asserted that the fat man was in no wise blamable; that he had run away on his own hook, and would do it again if he wanted to. But he broke there with a heavy sob; and the fat man said: "There! there! Cootsey, go along with the old 'un, and here's a dollar for you." And Tod cried aloud.

The good minister had brought a letter for him, too, and as the boy read it through his tears he turned homeward almost eagerly.

"Dear Tod," it ran: "I have been quite sick since you left me. You must come back, for I miss you, and I can never get well again without you. I've got a new kink on a pair of stilts I've made you, but I can't tell how long to make them till you come back. Fanny comes over every day, and talks about you so much I half believe sometimes she likes you better than she does her old sick uncle; but I can stand that, because you deserve it, and I'm too old for little girls to like very much. It'll soon be the Fourth, you know, and we must be getting ready for a big time. Come home at once, for I am waiting.

"To Stoddard Anderson, from his old friend and teacher."

TOD

Tod went home. He hastened to the teacher's darkened room. The dear old face had grown pale—so very pale! The kindly hand reached out to grasp the boy's was thin and wasted, and the gentle voice that he had learned to love was faint and low—so very low, it sounded like a prayer. The good minister turned silently and left the two old friends together; and there were teardrops in his eyes.

And so the little, staggering life went on alone. Some old woman gossip, peering through the eye of a needle on the institution known as the "Ladies' Benevolent Sewing Society," said that "it 'peared to her like that boy of the preacher's jest kep' a-pinin' and a-pinin' away like, ever sence they fetched him back from his runaway scrape. She'd seen him time and time again sence then, and although the little snipe was innocent-like to all appearances, she'd be bound that he was in devilment enough! Reckoned he was too proud to march in the school p'cession at the teacher's funer'l; and he didn't go to the meetin'-house at all, but putt off to the graveyard by hisse'f; and when they got there with the corpse, Tod was a-settin' with his legs a-hangin' in the grave, and a-pitchin' clods in, and a-smilin'. And only jest the other evening," she continued, "as I was comin' past there kindo' in the dusk-like, that boy was a-settin' a-straddle o' the grave, and jest a-cryin'! And I thought it kindo' strange-like, and stopped and hollered: 'What's the matter of ye, Tod?' and he ups and hollers back: 'Stumpt my toe, durn ye!' and thinks I, 'My youngster, they'll be a day o' reckonin' fer you!'"

The old world worried on, till July came at last, and with it that most glorious day that wrapped the baby nation in its swaddling-clothes of stripes and stars and laid it in the lap of Liberty. And what a day that was! and how the birds did sing that morning from the green tops of the trees when the glad sunlight came glancing through the jewelled leaves and woke them! And not more joyous were the birds, or more riotous their little throbbing hearts to "pipe the trail and cheep and twitter twenty million loves," than the merry children that came fluttering to the grove to join their revelry.

O brighter than a dream toward the boy that swung his hat from the tree-top near the brook swept the procession of children from the town. And he flushed with some strange ecstasy as he saw a little girl in white, with a wreath of evergreen, wave her crimson sash in answer to him, while the column slowly filed across the open bridge, where yet again he saw her reappear in the reflection in the stream below. Then, after the dull opening of prayer, and the more tedious exercises following, how the woods did ring with laughter; how the boys vied with one another in their labors of arranging swings and clearing underbrush away preparatory to a day of unconfined enjoyment; and how the girls shrieked to "see the black man coming," and how coquettishly they struggled when captured and carried off by that dread being, and yet what eagerness they displayed in his behalf! And "Ring"—men and women even joining in the game, and kissing one another's wives and husbands like mad. Why, even the ugly old gentleman, with a carbuncle on the back of his neck, grew riotous with mirth, and when tripped full length upon the sward by the little widow in half-mourning, bustled nimbly to his feet and kissed her, with some wicked pun about "grass" widows, that made him laugh till his face grew as red as his carbuncle. That bashful young man who had straggled off alone, sitting so uncomfortably upon a log, killing bugs and spiders, like an ugly giant with a monster club—how he must have envied the airy freedom of those "old boys and girls"!

Then there was a group of older men talking so long and earnestly about the weather and the crops that they had not discovered that the shade of the old beech they sat beneath had stolen silently away and left them sitting in the sun, and was even then performing its refreshing office for a big, sore-eyed dog, who, with panting jaws and lolling tongue, was winking away the lives of a swarm of gnats with the most stoical indifference.

And so time wore along till dinner came, and women, with big open baskets, bent above the snowy cloths spread out upon the grass, arranging "the substantials" and the dainties of a feast too varied and too toothsome for anything but epicurean memories to describe. And then the abandon of the voracious guests! No dainty affectations—no formality—no etiquette—no anything but the full sway of healthful appetites incited by the exhilarant exercises of the day into keenest rapacity and relish.

"Don't you think it's goin' to rain?" asked some one, suddenly. A little rosy-gilled gentleman, with the aid of a chicken-leg for a lever, raised his fat face skyward, and after a serious contemplation of the clouds, wouldn't say for certain whether it would rain or not, but informed the unfortunate querist, after pulling his head into its usual position and laying down the lever to make room for a bite of bread, that "if it didn't rain there'd be a long dry spell"; and then he snorted a mimic snow-storm of bread-crumbs on his vis-à-vis, who looked wronged, and said he "guessed he'd take another piece of that-air pie down there."

It was looking very much like rain by the time the dinner things were cleared away. Anxious mothers, with preserve-stains on their dresses, were running here and there with such exclamations to the men-folks as "Do hurry up!" and "For goodness sake, John, take the baby till I find my parasol," and "There, Thomas, don't lug that basket off till I find my pickle-dish!"

Already the girls had left the swings, which were being taken down, and were tying handkerchiefs over their hats and standing in despairing contemplation of the ruin of their dresses. Some one called from the stand for the ladies not to be at all alarmed, it wasn't going to rain, and there wasn't a particle of danger of ——; but there a clap of thunder interrupted, and went on growling menacingly, while a little girl, with her hair blown wildly over her bare shoulders, and with a face, which a moment before glowed like her crimson scarf, now whiter than her snowy dress, ran past the stand and fell fainting to the ground. "Is there a doctor on the grounds?" called a loud voice in the distance, and, without waiting for a response—"For God's sake, come here quick; a boy has fallen from the swing, and maybe killed himself!"

And then the crowd gathered round him there, men with white faces, and frightened women and little, shivering children.

"Whose boy is it?"

"Hush; here comes his father." And the good minister, with stark features and clinched hands, passed through the surging throng that closed behind him even as the waves on Pharaoh.

Did I say all were excited? Not all; for there was one calm face, though very pale—paler yet for being pillowed on the green grass and the ferns.

"You mustn't move me," the boy said when he could speak; "tell 'em to come here." He smiled and tried to lift and fold his arms about his father's neck. "Poor father! poor father!" as though speaking to himself, "I always loved you, father, only you'd never believe it—never believe it. Now you will. I'll see mother, now—mother. Don't cry—I'm hurt, and I don't cry. And I'll see the teacher, too. He said I would. He said we would always be together there. Where's Fanny? Tell her—tell her—" But that strange unending silence fell upon his lips, and as the dying eyes looked up and out beyond the sighing tree-tops, he smiled to catch a gleam of sunshine through the foolish cloud that tried so hard to weep.

A REMARKABLE MAN

A REMARKABLE MAN

In the early winter 1875, returning from a rather lengthy sojourn in the Buckeye State, where a Hoosier is scrutinized as critically as a splinter in the thumb of a near-sighted man, I mentally resolved that just as soon as the lazy engine dragging me toward home had poked its smutty nose into the selvedge of my native State, I would disembark, lift my voice, and shout for joy for being safely delivered out of a land of perpetual strangers.

This opportunity was afforded me at Union City—a fussy old-hen-of-a-town, forever clucking over its little brood of railroads, as though worried to see them running over the line, and bristling with the importance of its charge.

The place is not an attractive one, stepping from the train in the early dusk of a December evening; in fact, the immediate view of the town is almost entirely concealed by a big square-faced hotel, standing, as it were,

A REMARKABLE MAN

on the very platform, as though its "runners" were behind time, and it had come down to solicit its own custom. A walk of sixty steps, however, gave me a sweeping view of the main business street of the city; and here it was, by one of those rare freaks of circumstance, that I suddenly found myself standing face to face with an old friend. "Smith!" said I. "Correct!" said he, and all lacking to complete the tableau was the red light. And now, as my story has more to do with a more remarkable man than either Smith or myself, I shall hasten to that notable—only introducing humbler personages as necessity demands.

That night was a bragging, blustering, bullying sort of a night. The wind was mad—stark, staring mad; running over and around the town, howling and whooping like a maniac. It whirled and whizzed, and wheeled about and whizzed again. It pelted the pedestrian's face with dust that stung like sleet. It wrenched at the signs, and rattled the doors and windows till the lights inside shivered as with affright. The unfurled awnings fluttered and flapped over the deserted streets like monstrous bats or birds of prey; and, gritting their iron teeth, the shutters lunged and snapped at their fastenings convulsively. Such a night as we like to hide away from, and with a good cigar, a good friend, and a good

A REMARKABLE MAN

fire, talk of soothing things and dream. My friend and I were not so isolated, however, upon this occasion; for the suddenness of the storm had driven us, for shelter, into "Bowers's Emporium"; and, seated in the rear of the spacious and brightly illuminated store, we might almost "dream we dwelt in marble halls," were it not for the rather profuse display of merchandise and a voluminous complement of show-cards, reading "Bargains in Overcoats," "Best and Cheapest Underwear," "Buy Bowers's Boots!" etc.

The clerks were all idle, and employing their leisure in listening to a "fine-art" conversation, casually introduced by my friend remarking the extraordinary development of the bust and limbs of a *danseuse* on a paper collar-box; and after deploring the prostitution to which real talent was subjected, and satirizing the general degeneracy of modern art, he had drifted back to the rare old days of Hans Holbein, Albert Dürer, and that guild. And while dwelling enthusiastically upon the genius of Angelo, I became aware that among the listeners was a remarkable man. It was not his figure that impressed me, for that was of the ordinary mould, and rather shabbily attired in a tattered and ill-fitting coat of blue, sadly faded and buttonless; a short-waisted vest of no particular pattern, fastened together by means of a

A REMARKABLE MAN

loosened loop of binding pulled through a button-hole, and held to its place by a stumpy lead-pencil with a preponderance of rubber at the end; the pantaloons very baggy and fraying at the bottoms, as though in excessive sympathy with a pair of coarse, ungainly army shoes that wore the appearance of having been through "Sherman's march to the sea."

Not remarkable, I say, in these particulars, for since "tramping" has arrived at the dignity of a profession, such characteristics are by no means uncommon; but when taken in conjunction with a head and face that would have served as model for either Abraham, Isaac, or Jacob, in patriarchal cast of feature and flow of beard, it is no wonder that my fancy saw in the figure before me a remarkable man. He stood uncovered, and in an eager listening attitude, as though drinking every syllable to the very dregs. His eyes were large and lustrous, and with that dreamy, far-off look peculiar to that quality of mind that sees what is described, even though buried in Pompeiian ruins, or under the pyramids of Egypt.

He met my rather scrutinizing gaze with a friendly and forgiving expression—adding an intuitive affinity by a nestling of the palms one within the other and a genial friction indicative of warm impulse and openness, yet

A REMARKABLE MAN

withal suggesting a due subservience to my own free will to accept the same as token of genuine esteem and admiration.

I thought I read his character aright in fancying, "Here is a man of more than ordinary culture and refinement," and I determined, if it were possible, to know him better. When I took an early opportunity to refer to him for information he responded eagerly, and in so profuse and elegant a style of diction that I was surprised.

He referred to Angelo as "that master whose iron pencil painted language on lips of stone, and whose crudest works in clay might well outlive the marble monuments of modern art." He glanced from one topic to another with a grace and ease that not only betokened a true mastery of the language, but an inexhaustible fund of information; nor was it long ere my "stock in hand" had dwindled down to the insignificant "yes-and-of-course" verbosity that is not worth the giving away. He dwelt with particular fondness upon literature; frequently referring to me as to works I most admired, and pointing out the beauties and excellence of old authors —Shakespeare, Milton, Pope, Dryden, and a host of others long dead and gone, but whose works live on eternally. All these, as they were successively reviewed, he quoted in a manner that evinced a thorough knowledge of their worth.

At last, after no little artifice and strategy, I drew him to his own history, which, as he proceeded with, grew fantastically interesting. His father, passing rich, had educated him for the ministry; but the profession didn't suit him—or, rather, he didn't suit the profession; for, to be frank, he was rather inclined in his younger days to be a "graceless dog"; and so, when it became evident that he must shift for himself, more at the instigation of literary friends than from any ambition or choice, he had entered the journalistic field, beginning at the bottom of the ladder—the bottom—and gradually rising from the compositor's case to the very rung of editorial success—when there came a crash,—a flaw in the grain, my boy, a flaw in the grain—and that flaw— Well, no matter!—The noblest minds had toppled from the height, and crumbled to the merest debris of pauper intellect. The grandest tomb the finger of the nation could point out was glutted with such food. Did he not remember poor Prentice, and, in memory, recall him now as vividly as though but yesterday, entering the sanctum of the Louisville "Journal," with the old-time greeting: "Ah, Charles; ready for work, I see. Well, here am I—punctual as Death." And then, after a good stiff brandy, which he could hardly raise to his lips with both trembling hands, poor George! how he would dictate, so rapidly that he (Charles) could scarcely put it down, although a clever hand at writing in those days. Served as amanuensis for five years, and transcribed with his own hand, "'Tis Midnight's Holy Hour," at ten o'clock in the morning, and had the poem entire ready for the compositor at half-past. At such times it was nothing uncommon for George to say, "Well done, thou Good and Faithful! the big end of the day is left you to transcribe as your pleasure may dictate. Only bear in mind, I shall expect a little gem from your individual pen for to-morrow's issue!"

"And do you write?" I broke in abruptly.

"I used to write," he answered, as though loath to make the acknowledgment—"that is, I sometimes rode Pegasus as a groom might ride his master's horse—but my flights were never high—never high!"

"For what reason, may I inquire? Surely you had no lack of inspiration with such men as Prentice about you?"

"Ay, there's the rub!" he sighed, with a negative shake. "The association of great men does not always tend to develop genius; the more especially when one's subservient position revolutionizes him into a mere machine. Yet I found some time, of course, for verse-

A REMARKABLE MAN

making; and, chiefly owing to the kindly encouragement of Mr. Prentice, I 'gave to the world,' as he was pleased to say, many little poems; but those of them that survive to-day are vagrants, like myself, and drifting about at the mercy of the press." Here the old man sighed heavily and mechanically fumbled his pencil.

I was growing deeply interested in the strange character before me, and although the faces of the group smiled at me significantly, I was not to be beguiled from my new acquaintance.

"There is a question," said I, "I would like to ask you, since from actual experience you are doubtless well informed upon it:—I have often heard it argued that the best productions of authors—poets in particular—are written under the influence of what they are pleased to term 'inspiration'; can you enlighten me as to the truth of that assertion?"

"I can say in reply," said the old man, with his unwavering eyes fixed upon mine—"I can say in reply that the best productions of authors—poets in particular—*are* written under the influence of what they are pleased to term 'inspiration.' I have seen it proved."

"How proved?" I asked.

"Listen. Take, for example, an instance I will cite: A man worn and enfeebled by age, whose eyes are dimmed to sightlessness almost; whose mind, once clear and vivid as the light of day, is now wavering and fickle as the wind: and yet at times this influence comes upon him like an avalanche, and as irresistible; a voice cries, 'Write! write! write!' nor does he know, when he has obeyed that summons, what his trembling hand has written. Further, that this is divine inspiration, his fragmentary productions will oftentimes be in the exact manner and diction of writers long since passed away; and I am satisfied they are produced at the direct dictation of the departed. I know this!"

"You astonish me," said I, in unfeigned wonder; "you say you know this—how do you know it?"

"Because I am the man."

Although the assertion, in my mind, was simply preposterous, there was a certain majesty in the utterance that held me half in awe. I looked upon him as one might look upon some curious being from an unknown world. He was moving now—pacing grotesquely up and down a little space of half a dozen steps, and wheeling, at the limits of his walk, as nimbly as the harlequin in the pantomime, and repeating, as though to himself, "I am the man; I am the man."

"Well, sir," said I, forcing myself into an air of indifference I did not feel—"well, sir, not for a moment questioning your own belief as to this strange influence which may possess you at times, you will pardon me for expressing the vaguest scepticism, since I have never been so fortunate as to witness an actual demonstration." He was about to interrupt me, but I continued coolly, "By what circumstance is this influence introduced—or how produced—is it—"

He broke in on me with a keen little pang of a laugh that almost made me shudder. "You are my convert," he exclaimed excitedly. "Quick! Give me paper—give me paper!" But before I could take my note-book from my pocket he had hurriedly snatched a scrap of wrapping-paper from the counter, and bending over it, was writing with great rapidity.

His manner was decidedly singular. In the occasional pauses he would make he would lean his forehead in the palm of his left hand, with the fingers dancing nervously upon the bald spot on the summit of his head, while with the hand that held the pencil he kept up a continued rotary movement in the air. Then he would suddenly pounce down upon the paper before him as though in a perfect frenzy of delight, and line after line would appear as if by magic, each succeeding one preluded by that sharp little yelp of a laugh: and ere three minutes had elapsed, he had covered both sides of the paper.

A REMARKABLE MAN

He then threw down his pencil, as though reluctantly, pushed me the scrap and motioned me to read.

I was at first completely mystified, for what I had confidently expected to be rhyme was prose; but ere I had examined it far I was as highly gratified as at first disappointed. The writing, although so recklessly scrawled, was quite legible, and here and there gave evidence of more than ordinary grace and elegance; the punctuation, so far as I was able to judge, seemed perfect in every part; and, in fact, the entire production bore the appearance of having been executed by a skilful hand.

I copy it verbatim from the original scrap, which now lies before me:

By this time they had come upon the figure of the old hag, seated by the roadside, and, in a harsh, cracked voice, crooning a dismal ballad. "By God's rood," quoth the knight, in a burst of admiration, "did I not tell thee 'twas some fair princess, decoyed from her father's castle and thus transformed, through the despicable arts of some wicked enchanter; for thou hast but to perk an ear to have the sense of hearing bathed and overflowed with melody. Dost thou not also note rare grace and sweetest dignity voiced, as it were, from the very tatters that enclothe her form?" "Indeed thou mayest," said the squire; "for I have heard it said 'rags may enfold the purest gold.'— Yet in this instance I am restrained to think it more like the hidalgo's dinner—'very little meat and a good deal of tablecloth.'" "Hold thy peace, bladderhead," exclaimed the knight, "lest I make thee gnaw thy words with loosened teeth. Listen what liquid syllables are spilled upon the atmosphere:"

> 'My father's halls, so rich and rare,
> Are desolate and bleak and bare;
> My father's heart and halls are one,
> Since I, their life and light, am gone.
>
> 'O, valiant knight, with hand of steel
> And heart of gold, hear my appeal:
> Release me from the spoiler's charms,
> And bear me to my father's arms.'

The knight had by this time thrown himself from his steed, and with lance reversed and visor doffed he sank upon his knees in the slime and ooze of the dike, exclaiming: "Be of good heart, fair princess! Thy succor is at hand, since the Fates have woven thee—the pearl of pearls—into the warp and woof of my great destiny. Nay, nay! No thanks! Thy father's beaming eye alone shall be my guerdon, for home thou shalt go, even though I must needs truckle thee thither on a barrow."

"Good," said I, grasping the old man by the hand. "Hail, Cervantes!"

"Cervantes? Cervantes?" he mused, as though bewildered; "why, what have I been writing? Is it not poetry?"

"Yes," I replied enthusiastically, "both prose and

poetry, and that of the rarest school. Read for yourself."

I handed him the scrap, but he pushed it from him with a gesture of impatience. "I told you once I could not read it, nor do I know what I have written. Read it aloud."

Although I hastened to comply, I did it with a decided air of incredulity as to the belief that he did not already know every word of it, and even closed with the gratuitous comment that I felt assured the quotation was perfect in every particular.

"Quotation!" repeated the old man, commiseratively; "quotation! Were you as well versed in such works, my son, as you led me at first to presume, you would know at once that not a single line of that occurs in 'Don Quixote,' although I do grant that I am the humble instrument through which the great Cervantes has just spoken." With this remark, delivered in a half-rebuking, half-compassionate tone, he stood milking his beard and blinking at the chandelier.

I acknowledged my error, and asked pardon for the insinuation, which I begged he would believe was not intended to offend; and that, upon second thought, I was satisfied that no such matter did exist in the printed history, which fact. I have since proved by a thorough investigation.

It required, however, considerable inventive tact and show of admiration to counteract the effect of my indiscreet remark; and not was this effectually accomplished until I had incidentally discovered a marked resemblance of his brow to Shakespeare's, which, by actual measurement, I found to correspond to a fraction with the measurement of the mask of that illustrious bard, as furnished by an exhaustive article I had seen a short time previous in one of our magazines.

This happily brought about the result I so much longed for, as I was extremely desirous of a further opportunity in which to study the character of this remarkable man. "Ah, Shakespeare!" said he, in a burst of genuine eloquence,—"there was a mind the gods endowed with wisdom ages have yet to learn; for bright and lustrous as it shines to-day—the Morning Star of human intellect —its glittering purity has yet a million million dawns, each brighter than the last. Its chastened rays are yet to blaze and radiate the darkened ways— Hold! My pencil! Quick—quick!"

He snatched at the paper wildly, and bending over it, began writing with a vindictiveness of effort that was alarming. He slashed the *t*'s and stabbed the punctuation-points savagely. The writing continued, interspersed occasionally with a pause in which he would flourish his pencil like a dripping sword, only to be plunged again and again into the quivering breast of its victim. Finally he dashed it down, pushed the paper from him as one would spurn a vanquished enemy, and sank, limp and exhausted, into a chair. I snatched up the paper eagerly, and read:

> *Falstaff.* I call him dog, forsooth, because he snarls—
> Snarls, d'ye hear?—and laves his rabid fangs
> In slobber-froth that drips in slimy gouts
> Of venomous slander. Out upon the cur!
> He sets his mangy foot upon the sod,
> And grass grows rank and withers at the touch,
> And tangles into wiry thatch for snakes
> To spawn beneath. The very air he breathes
> Becomes a poison gas, and generates
> Disease and pestilence. Would he were here,
> That I might whet my sword against his ribs,
> Although his rotten, putrid soul unhoused
> Would breed a stench worse than my barber's breath.
> The dog! The damnable—
>
> *Pistol.* Hist! here he comes!
> God's body! master, has he overheard,
> 'Tis cock-crow with thy ghost!
>
> (*Enter Poins.*) How now, my Jack—
> Prince ass of Jacks, methought I heard thee bray.

A REMARKABLE MAN

Falstaff. Ay, well and marry! for this varlet here
Deserves more brays than praise, the scurvy dog!
Good lack! thou might'st have heard me call him dog
A pebble's toss from this; but now that thou art come,
My dagger-points of wrath do melt away
Before thy genial smile as icicles
Might ooze to nothingness at summer noon.
That other flask, you dog! and have a care
Thou handle it more gently than the first,
Lest I, as thou didst it, thy noddle burst."

Although expecting something after the Shakespearian school, I was not prepared for this, and in reading it aloud I actually found myself endeavoring to imitate the stage manner of Hackett, whom years ago I had seen in "King Henry IV" at the old Metropolitan, Indianapolis. "Ah!" said the old man, "you are more familiar with that, I see. Tell me, have you ever seen those lines in 'Shakespeare'?" There was such a look of conscious triumph in his face, so self-satisfied an expression, that I—although half believing I was in some way being duped—could but reply that I was most thoroughly convinced the lines did not occur in any of the works of that great master.

"They do not," said the old man, briefly.

"But how," said I, "is it possible for you to so perfectly imitate his style, not only in language, but theme, expression, force, character, grotesqueness—"

"Stop, my son; stop!" he broke in.—"Must I again remind you that it is not imitation: I take no credit to myself—how dare I when in writing thus my individual mind is gone, simply chaotic? It is not imitation; it is Shakespeare."

I could venture no further comment without fear of offending, and he already stood as though hesitating to depart.

"Stay, then," said I, "until I see a further exercise of this marvellous power you possess. Here, sit down, rest awhile; you seem almost exhausted."

"I am nearly so," he replied, "but there is no rest for me until this influence is entirely subsided. No rest for me yet; no rest! no rest!"

He was again pacing his old walk, now like a weary sentinel, and I thought as I gazed upon him, "What riddle of the human kind is this?" Over and over again came the question; and over and over an old rhyme I had somewhere read, mockingly responded—

"Rain, rain, and sun! a rainbow in the sky!
A young man will be wiser by and by;
An old man's wit may wander ere he die."

A REMARKABLE MAN

And lulled by the mild monotony of this, I was fast drifting into a dreamy train of thought, when the old man halted suddenly, and with one elbow leaning on the counter and his head resting on his hand, he began humming a tune—a strangely sweet and tender air; low, and just a little harsh at first and indistinct, but welling softly into cadence wonderfully rich and pure; then quavering again in minor swoons of melody so delicately beautiful I can but liken the effect produced to that ethereal mystery of sound unravelled from the zithern by a master hand,—

"A slender thread of song in saddest tune."

I had leaned forward with my own head resting in my hand, that I might the better listen, and was not aware, until the song abruptly ended, that the old man had been writing as he sang.

"There," said he, handing me the scrap, "you have heard the tune; here are the words, perhaps."

It may have been a very foolish thing, it may have been weak and womanish, yet as my eyes bent over it and read, the lines grew curiously blurred toward the last; nor did I guess the cause until a tear—a great ripe teardrop—fell upon my hand. And, reader, could I present

A REMARKABLE MAN

the song to you just as it came to me, with all the strange surroundings—the stranger experience of the hour; the solemn silence of the group; the wailing of the wind outside as though the world, weary of itself, could only sigh, sigh, sigh!—could I prelude it with that low, sweet murmuring of melody that haunts me even now, your own eyes needs must moisten as you read:

THE HARP OF THE MINSTREL

The harp of the minstrel has never a tone
    As sad as the song in his bosom to-night,
For the magical touch of his fingers alone
    Cannot waken the echoes that breathe it aright;
But oh! as the smile of the moon may impart
    A sorrow to one in an alien clime,
Let the light of the melody fall on the heart,
    And cadence his grief into musical rhyme.

The faces have faded, the eyes have grown dim
    That once were his passionate love and his pride;
And alas! all the smiles that once blossomed for him
    Have fallen away as the flowers have died.
The hands that entwined him the laureate's wreath
    And crowned him with fame in the long, long ago,
Like the laurels are withered and folded beneath
    The grass and the stubble—the frost and the snow.

A REMARKABLE MAN

> Then sigh, if thou wilt, as the whispering strings
>   Strive ever in vain for the utterance clear,
> And think of the sorrowful spirit that sings,
>   And jewel the song with the gem of a tear.
> For the harp of the minstrel has never a tone
>   As sad as the song in his bosom to-night,
> And the magical touch of his fingers alone
>   Cannot waken the echoes that breathe it aright.

I had read the lines over to myself, and although recognizing many touches decidedly like those of the famous author of Lalla Rookh, I was not wholly satisfied with the production; and it struck me with peculiar force that an ethereal composition would surely not be so lavishly tinctured with unutterable sorrow—aside from being far inferior to a hundred earthly songs of Moore's. So, with this argument for my weapon, I determined to conquer the superstition that had almost overpowered me. I had noticed, too, in both former instances a singular fact: The old man, though so ready to fend off all comment that might reflect a single ray of praise upon himself, listened with more of the air of a critic than one whose interest was merely that of curiosity, and still when the fragmentary productions were read aloud, a look of more than ordinary satisfaction would lighten up his eyes. These facts, hastily reviewed, determined me upon a course of action I had instant opportunity to adopt.

"Read it aloud," said the old man, impatiently; "read it aloud!"

I complied with more than usual enthusiasm, reading verbatim from the copy, until I came to the repetition of the first four lines, which I thus transposed, or, rather, paraphrased.

> "The harp of the minstrel has never a *note*
> As sad as the song in his bosom *expressed*,
> And the magical touch of his fingers *afloat*
> *Drifts over the echoes that sleep in the breast.*"

This I was careful to deliver without emphasis or mark of any kind by which he might discover any imposition on my part. As I closed I stole a hasty glance at his face, and was gratified to find it wearing a rather startled expression: not only did his features betray a puzzled and questioning air, but his hand was mechanically extended, as though reaching for the paper in my own.

"Do you want to see it?" I asked suddenly, handing him the scrap.

"Yes, I—Oh, no—no," he broke in, dropping his hand, and his face coloring vividly; but turning again as quickly, he added: "Yes, give it to me. Where are the others? I must be going."

A REMARKABLE MAN

"Why must you go?" I asked, still retaining the scrap; "I had hoped—"

"I am going!" he interrupted, brusquely, snatching up the scraps that lay upon the counter, and reaching for the one I still held. "Give me the poem. I will trouble you no longer."

"Allow me to retain it, I beg of you," said I, with a significant smile, and the slightest tinge of sarcasm in my voice. "Let me keep it as a befitting memento of the 'inspiration' I have seen so potently exercised."

His face was pale with anger as he replied:

"I will not. When you want rhyme write it yourself.— You can at least write *doggerel*."

"Very neat," said I, laughing. "We understand each other, so let's be friends. Here is my hand and a dollar besides. Give me the other scraps—I want them all."

I took them from him as he clutched at the bill, which he smothered in his palm, and turned away without a word.

"Here, Charley," called one of the bystanders, "half of that's enough for you to-night."

The door slammed violently and he was gone.

"Old Cain will have that dollar in just five minutes," continued the man.

"And who's Old Cain?" I asked.

"Keeps the doggery just over the line."

A REMARKABLE MAN

"Old Charley" M—— is a well-known character in Union City—his home, in fact, although he often disappears for long periods, but, as my informant remarked, "always turns up again like a bad penny."

His story of his early life is at least based upon the truth, but now so highly colored it is a decidedly difficult matter to detect that simple element.

Originally he was a printer, but early abandoned that vocation for another, and that in turn for another, and so on, until by easy gradations he had become, as the old saw has it, "Jack of all trades and master of none."

Among his many accomplishments he is a musician of considerable skill—plays the flute, violin, and guitar—all quite passably; is a great reader, a fine conversationalist—which accomplishment I personally vouch for. But chief of all his accomplishments is that of writing clever imitations of the old authors and poets. These productions he prepares with great care, commits them to memory, and is ready to dispose of them by as ingenious a method.

And yet, although he be a vagabond; although his friends—such as they are—are first to call him sot; although the selfish world that hurries past may jostle him unnoticed from the path; and although he styles himself a "graceless dog,"—in all candor, and in justice to my true belief, I call him a remarkable man.

A NEST-EGG

A NEST-EGG

BUT a few miles from the city here, and on the sloping banks of the stream noted more for its plenitude of "chubs" and "shiners" than the gamier two- and four-pound bass for which, in season, so many credulous anglers flock and lie in wait, stands a country residence, so convenient to the stream, and so inviting in its pleasant exterior and comfortable surroundings—barn, dairy, and spring-house—that the weary, sunburnt, and disheartened fisherman, out from the dusty town for a day of recreation, is often wont to seek its hospitality. The house in style of architecture is something of a departure from the typical farm-house, being designed and fashioned with no regard to symmetry or proportion, but rather, as is suggested, built to conform to the matter-of-fact and most sensible ideas of its owner, who, if it pleased him, would have small windows where large ones ought to be, and vice versa, whether they balanced properly to the eye or not. And chimneys—he would have as many as he wanted, and no two alike, in either height or size. And if he wanted the front of the house turned from all possible view, as though abashed at any chance of public scrutiny, why, that was his affair and not the public's; and, with like perverseness, if he chose to thrust his kitchen under the public's very nose, what should the generally fagged-out, half-famished representative of that dignified public do but reel in his dead minnow, shoulder his fishing-rod, clamber over the back fence of the old farm-house and inquire within, or jog back to the city, inwardly anathematizing that very particular locality or the whole rural district in general. That is just the way that farm-house looked to the writer of this sketch one week ago—so individual it seemed—so liberal, and yet so independent. It wasn't even weather-boarded, but, instead, was covered smoothly with some cement, as though the plasterers had come while the folks were visiting, and so, unable to get at the interior, had just plastered the outside.

I am more than glad that I was hungry enough, and weary enough, and wise enough to take the house at its first suggestion; for, putting away my fishing-tackle for the morning, at least, I went up the sloping bank, crossed the dusty road, and confidently clambered over the fence.

A NEST-EGG

Not even a growling dog to intimate that I was trespassing. All was open—gracious-looking—pastoral. The sward beneath my feet was velvet-like in elasticity, and the scarce visible path I followed through it led promptly to the open kitchen door. From within I heard a woman singing some old ballad in an undertone, while at the threshold a trim, white-spurred rooster stood poised on one foot, curving his glossy neck and cocking his wattled head as though to catch the meaning of the words. I paused. It was a scene I felt restrained from breaking in upon, nor would I, but for the sound of a strong male voice coming around the corner of the house:

"Sir. Howdy!"

Turning, I saw a rough-looking but kindly featured man of sixty-five, the evident owner of the place.

I returned his salutation with some confusion and much deference. "I must really beg your pardon for this intrusion," I began, "but I have been tiring myself out fishing, and your home here looked so pleasant—and I felt so thirsty—and—"

"Want a drink, I reckon," said the old man, turning abruptly toward the kitchen door, then pausing as suddenly, with a backward motion of his thumb——"jest foller the path here down to the little brick—that's the spring—and you'll find 'at you've come to the right place fer drinkin'-worter! Hold on a minute tel I git you a tumbler—there're nothin' down there but a tin."

"Then don't trouble yourself any further," I said, heartily, "for I'd rather drink from a tin cup than a goblet of pure gold."

"And so'd I," said the old man, reflectively, turning mechanically, and following me down the path. "'Druther drink out of a tin—er jest a fruit-can with the top knocked off—er—er—er a gourd," he added in a zestful, reminiscent tone of voice, that so heightened my impatient thirst that I reached the spring-house fairly in a run.

"Well-sir!" exclaimed my host, in evident delight, as I stood dipping my nose in the second cupful of the cool, revivifying liquid, and peering in a congratulatory kind of way at the blurred and rubicund reflection of my features in the bottom of the cup, "well-sir, blame-don! ef it don't do a feller good to see you enjoyin' of it thataway! But don't you drink too much o' the worter! —'cause there're some sweet milk over there in one o' them crocks, maybe; and ef you'll jest, kindo' keerful-like, lift off the led of that third one, say, over there to yer left, and dip you out a tinful er two o' that, w'y, it'll do you good to drink it, and it'll do me good to see you at it— But hold up!—hold up!" he called, abruptly, as, nowise loath, I bent above the vessel designated. "Hold yer hosses fer a second! Here's Marthy; let her git it fer ye."

If I was at first surprised and confused, meeting the master of the house, I was wholly startled and chagrined in my present position before its mistress. But as I arose, and stammered, in my confusion, some incoherent apology, I was again reassured and put at greater ease by the comprehensive and forgiving smile the woman gave me, as I yielded her my place, and, with lifted hat, awaited her further kindness.

"I came just in time, sir," she said, half laughingly, as with strong, bare arms she reached across the gurgling trough and replaced the lid that I had partially removed.—"I came just in time, I see, to prevent father from having you dip into the 'morning's-milk,' which, of course, has scarcely a veil of cream over the face of it as yet. But men, as you are doubtless willing to admit," she went on jocularly, "don't know about these things. You must pardon father, as much for his well-meaning ignorance of such matters, as for this cup of cream, which I am sure you will better relish."

She arose, still smiling, with her eyes turned frankly on my own. And I must be excused when I confess that as I bowed my thanks, taking the proffered cup and lifting it to my lips, I stared with an uncommon interest and pleasure at the donor's face.

She was a woman of certainly not less than forty years of age. But the figure, and the rounded grace and fulness of it, together with the features and the eyes, completed as fine a specimen of physical and mental health as ever it has been my fortune to meet; there was something so full of purpose and resolve—something so wholesome, too, about the character—something so womanly—I might almost say manly, and would, but for the petty prejudice maybe occasioned by the trivial fact of a locket having dropped from her bosom as she knelt; and that trinket still dangles in my memory even as it then dangled and dropped back to its concealment in her breast as she arose. But her face, by no means handsome in the common meaning, was marked with a breadth and strength of outline and expression that approached the heroic—a face that once seen is forever fixed in memory —a personage once met one must know more of. And so it was, that an hour later, as I strolled with the old man about his farm, looking, to all intents, with the profoundest interest at his Devonshires, Shorthorns, Jerseys, and the like, I lured from him something of an outline of his daughter's history.

"There're no better girl 'n Marthy!" he said, mechanically answering some ingenious allusion to her worth. "And yit," he went on reflectively, stooping from his seat in the barn door and with his open jack-knife picking up a little chip with the point of the blade—"and yit—you wouldn't believe it—but Marthy was the oldest o' three daughters, and hed—I may say—hed more advantages o' marryin'—and yit, as I was jest goin' to say, she's the very one 'at didn't marry. Hed every advantage—Marthy did. W'y, we even hed her educated—her mother was a-livin' then—and we was well enough fixed to afford the educatin' of her, mother allus contended— and we was—besides, it was Marthy's notion, too, and you know how women is thataway when they git their head set. So we sent Marthy down to Indianop'lus, and got her books and putt her in school there, and paid fer her keepin' and ever'thing; and she jest—well, you may say, lived there stiddy fer better'n four year. O' course she'd git back ever' once-an-a-while, but her visits was allus, some-way-another, onsatisfactory-like, 'cause, you see, Marthy was allus my favorite, and I'd allus laughed and told her 'at the other girls could git married ef they wanted, but *she* was goin' to be the 'nest-egg' of our family, and 'slong as I lived I wanted her at home with me. And she'd laugh and contend 'at she'd as lif be an old maid as not, and never expected to marry, ner didn't want to. But she had me sceart onc't, though! Come out from the city one time, durin' the army, with a peart-lookin' young feller in blue clothes and gilt straps on his shoulders. Young lieutenant he was—name o' Morris. Was layin' in camp there in the city somers. I disremember which camp it was now adzackly—but anyway, it 'peared like he had plenty o' time to go and come, fer from that time on he kep' on a-comin'—ever' time Marthy 'ud come home, he'd come, too; and I got to noticin' 'at Marthy come home a good 'eal more'n she used to afore Morris first brought her. And blame ef the thing didn't git to worryin' me! And onc't I spoke to mother about it, and told her ef I thought the feller wanted to marry Marthy I'd jest stop his comin' right then and there. But mother she sorto' smiled and said somepin' 'bout men a-never seein' through nothin'; and when I ast her what she meant, w'y, she ups and tells me 'at Morris didn't keer nothin' fer Marthy, ner Marthy fer Morris, and then went on to tell me that Morris was kindo' aidgin' up to'rds Annie—she was next to Marthy, you know, in pint of years and experience, but ever'body allus said 'at Annie was the purtiest one o' the whole three of 'em. And so when mother told me 'at the signs pinted to'rds Annie, w'y, of course, I hedn't no particular objections to that, 'cause Morris was of good fambly

A NEST-EGG

enough it turned out, and, in fact, was as stirrin' a young feller as ever I'd want fer a son-in-law, and so I hed nothin' more to say—ner they wasn't no occasion to say nothin', 'cause right along about then I begin to notice 'at Marthy quit comin' home so much, and Morris kep' a-comin' more. Tel finally, one time he was out here all by hisself, 'long about dusk, come out here where I was feedin', and ast me, all at onc't, and in a straightfor'ard way, ef he couldn't marry Annie; and, some-way-another, blame ef it didn't make me as happy as him when I told him yes! You see that thing proved, pine-blank, 'at he wasn't a-fishin' round fer Marthy. Well-sir, as luck would hev it, Marthy got home about a half-hour later, and I'll give you my word I was never so glad to see the girl in my life! It was foolish in me, I reckon, but when I see her drivin' up the lane—it was purt' nigh dark then, but I could see her through the open winder from where I was settin' at the supper-table, and so I jest quietly excused myself, p'lite-like, as a feller will, you know, when they's comp'ny round, and I slipped off and met her jest as she was about to git out to open the barn gate. 'Hold up, Marthy,' says I; 'set right where you air; I'll open the gate fer you, and I'll do anything else fer you in the world 'at you want me to!'

"'W'y, what's pleased *you* so?' she says, laughin', as

A NEST-EGG

she druv through slow-like and a-ticklin' my nose with the cracker of the buggy-whip.—'What's pleased *you?*'

"'Guess,' says I, jerkin' the gate to, and turnin' to lift her out.

"'The new peanner's come?' says she, eager-like.

"'Yer new peanner's come,' says I, 'but that's not it.'

"'Strawberries fer supper?' says she.

"'Strawberries fer supper,' says I; 'but that ain't it.'

"Jest then Morris's hoss whinnied in the barn, and she glanced up quick and smilin' and says, 'Somebody come to see somebody?'

"'You're a-gittin' warm,' says I.

"'Somebody come to see *me?*' she says, anxious-like.

"'No,' says I, 'and I'm glad of it—fer this one 'at's come wants to git married, and o' course I wouldn't harber in my house no young feller 'at was a-layin' round fer a chance to steal away the "Nest-egg,"' says I, laughin'.

"Marthy had riz up in the buggy by this time, but as I helt up my hands to her, she sorto' drawed back a minute, and says, all serious-like and kindo' whisperin':

"'Is it *Annie?*'

"I nodded. 'Yes,' says I, 'and what's more, I've give my consent, and mother's give hern—the thing's all settled. Come, jump out and run in and be happy with the rest of us!' and I helt out my hands ag'in, but she didn't 'pear to take no heed. She was kindo' pale, too, I thought, and swallered a time er two like as ef she couldn't speak plain.

"'Who is the man?' she ast.

"'Who—who's the man,' I says, a-gittin' kindo' out o' patience with the girl.—'W'y, you know who it is, o' course.—It's Morris,' says I. 'Come, jump down! Don't you see I'm waitin' fer ye?'

"'Then take me,' she says; and blame-don! ef the girl didn't keel right over in my arms as limber as a rag! Clean fainted away! Honest! Jest the excitement, I reckon, o' breakin' it to her so suddent-like—'cause she liked Annie, I've sometimes thought, better'n even she did her own mother. Didn't go half so hard with her when her other sister married. Yes-sir!" said the old man, by way of sweeping conclusion, as he rose to his feet—"Marthy's the on'y one of 'em 'at never married—both the others is gone—Morris went all through the army and got back safe and sound—'s livin' in Idyho, and doin' fust-rate. Sends me a letter ever' now and then. Got three little chunks o' grandchildern out there, and I' never laid eyes on one of 'em. You see, I'm a-gittin' to be quite a middle-aged man—in fact, a very middle-aged man, you might say. Sence mother died, which has be'n

—lem-me-see—mother's be'n dead somers in the neighberhood o' ten year.—Sence mother died I've be'n a-gittin' more and more o' *Marthy's* notion—that is,—you couldn't ever hire *me* to marry nobody! and them has allus be'n and still is the 'Nest-egg's' views! Listen! That's her a-callin' fer us now. You must sorto' overlook the freedom, but I told Marthy you'd promised to take dinner with us to-day, and it 'ud never do to disappint her now. Come on." And ah! it would have made the soul of you either rapturously glad or madly envious to see how meekly I consented.

I am always thinking that I never tasted coffee till that day; I am always thinking of the crisp and steaming rolls, ored over with the molten gold that hinted of the clover-fields, and the bees that had not yet permitted the honey of the bloom and the white blood of the stalk to be divorced; I am always thinking that the young and tender pullet we happy three discussed was a near and dear relative of the gay patrician rooster that I first caught peering so inquisitively in at the kitchen door; and I am always—always thinking of "The Nest-egg."

TALE OF A SPIDER

TALE OF A SPIDER

FIRST—I want it most distinctly understood that I am superstitious, notwithstanding the best half of my life, up to the very present, has been spent in the emphatic denial of that fact. And I am painfully aware that this assertion at so late a date can but place my former character in a most unenviable light; yet for reasons *you* will never know, I have, with all due deliberation, determined to hold the truth up stark and naked to the world, with the just acknowledgment, shorn of all attempt at palliation or excuse, that for the best half of my life I have been simply a coward and a liar.

Second—From a careful and impartial study of my fellow-beings, I have arrived at the settled conviction that nine men of every ten are just as superstitious as myself; yet, with the difference, that, for reasons *I* know, they refuse to openly acknowledge it, many of them dodging the admission even within their own ever curious and questioning minds.

Third—Most firmly fixed in this belief and intuitively certain of at least the inner confidence and sympathy of a grand majority of those who read, I throw aside all personal considerations, defy all ridicule—all reason, if you like—for the purpose wholly to devote myself to the narration of an actual experience that for three long weeks has been occurring with me nightly in this very room. You should hear me laugh about it in the daytime! Oh, I snap my fingers then, and whistle quite as carelessly and scornfully as you doubtless would; but at night—at night—and it's night now—I grow very, very serious somehow, and put all raillery aside, and all in vain here argue by the hour that it's nothing in the world but the baleful imaginings of a feverish mind, and the convulsive writhings of a dyspeptic fancy. But enough!—Even forced to admit that I'm a fool, I will tell my story.

Although by no means of a morbid or misanthropic disposition, the greater portion of my time I occupy in strict seclusion, here at my desk—for only when alone can I conscientiously indulge certain propensities of thinking aloud, talking to myself, leaping from my chair occasionally to dance a new thought round the room, or take it in my arms, and hug and hold and love it as I would a great, fat, laughing baby with a bunch of jingling keys.

Then there are times, too, when worn with work, and I find my pen dabbling by the wayside in sluggish blots of ink, that I delight to take up the old guitar which leans here in the corner, and twang among the waltzes that I used to know, or lift a most unlovely voice in half-forgotten songs whose withered notes of melody fall on me like dead leaves, but whose crisp rustling still has power to waken from "the dusty crypt of darkened forms and faces" the glad convivial spirits that once thronged about me in the wayward past, and made my young life one long peal of empty merriment. Someway, I've lost the knack of wholesome laughter now, and for this reason, maybe, I so often find my fingers tangled in the strings of my guitar; for, after all, there is an indefinable something in the tone of a guitar that is not all of earth. I have often fancied that departed friends came back to hide themselves away in this old husk of song that we might pluck them forth to live again in quavering tones of tenderness and love and minor voices of remembrance that coax us on to heaven. Pardon my vagaries.—I'm practical enough at times; at times I fail. But I must be clear to-night; I must be, and I will.

TALE OF A SPIDER

This night three weeks ago I had worked late, though on a task involving nothing that could possibly have warped my mind to an unnatural state, other than that of peculiar wakefulness; for although physically needful of rest, I felt that it was useless to retire; and so I wheeled my sofa in a cosey position near the stove, lighted a cigar (my chum Hays had left me four hours previous), and flinging myself down in languid pose best suiting the requirements of an aimless reverie, I resigned all serious complexities of thought and was wholly comfortable.

The silence of the night without was deep. Not a footstep in the street below, and not a sound of any living earthly thing fell on the hearing, though that sense was whetted to such acuteness I could plainly hear the ticking of a clock somewhere across the street.

All things about the room were in their usual order. My letters on the desk were folded as I answered them, and filed away; my books were ranged in order, and my manuscripts tucked out of sight and mind, and no scrap of paper to remind me of my never-ended work, save the blank sheet that always lies in readiness for me to pounce upon with any vagrant thought that comes along, and close beside it the open inkstand and the idle pen.

I had reclined thus in utter passiveness of mind for

TALE OF A SPIDER

half an hour, perhaps, when suddenly I heard, or thought I heard, below me in the street, the sound of some stringed instrument. I rose up on my elbow and listened. Some serenader, I guessed. Yes, I could hear it faintly, but so far away it seemed, and indistinct, I was uncertain. I arose, went to the window, raised it and leaned out; but as the sound grew fainter and failed entirely, I closed the window and sat down again; but even as I did so the mysterious tones fell on my hearing plainer than before. I listened closely, and though little more than a ghost of sound, I still could hear, and quite audibly distinguish, the faint repeated twanging of the six open strings of a guitar—so plainly, indeed, that I instinctively recognized the irritating fact that both the "E" and "D" strings were slightly out of tune. I turned with some strange impulse to my own instrument, and I must leave the reader to imagine the cold thrill of surprise and fear that crept over me as the startling conviction slowly dawned upon my mind that the sounds came from that unlooked-for quarter. The guitar was leaning in its old position in the corner, the face turned to the wall, and although I confess it with reluctance, full five minutes elapsed before I found sufficient courage to approach and pick it up; then I came near dropping it in abject terror as a great, fat, blowzy spider ran across my hand and went scampering up the wall. What do you think of spiders, anyhow? You say "Wooh!" I say you don't know anything about spiders.

I examined first the wall to see if there might not be some natural cause for the mysterious sounds—some open crevice for the wind, some loosened and vibrating edge of paper, or perhaps a bristle protruding from the plaster—but I found no evidence that could in any way afford an answer to the perplexing query. An old umbrella and a broom stood in the corner, but in neither of these inanimate objects could I find the vaguest explanation of the problem that so wholly and entirely possessed me.

I could not have been mistaken. It was no trick of fancy—no hallucination. I had not only listened to the sounds repeated, over and over, a dozen times at least, but I had recognized and measured the respective values of the tones, and as I turned, half in awe, took up the instrument and lightly swept the strings, the positive proof for the conviction jarred as discordantly upon my fancy as upon my ears.—The two strings, "E" and "D," were out of tune.

I will no longer attempt the detail of my perturbed state of curiosity and the almost dazed condition of my mind; such an effort would at best be vain. But

TALE OF A SPIDER

I sat down, doggedly, at last; and in a spirit of indifference the most defiant I could possibly assume, I ran the guitar up to a keen, exultant key, and dashed off into a quickstep that made the dumb old echoes of the room leap up and laugh with melody. I was determined in my own mind to stave off the most unwholesome influence that seemed settling fog-like over me; and as the sharp twang of the strings rang out upon the night, and the rich vibrating chords welled up and overflowed the silence like a flood, the embers of old-time enthusiasm kindled in my heart and flamed up in a warmth of real delight. Suddenly, in the midst of this rapturous outburst, as with lifted face I stared ceilingward, my eyes again fell on that horrid spider, madly capering about the wall in a little circumference of a dozen inches, perhaps, wheeling and whirling up and down, and round and round again, as though laboring under some wild, jubilant excitement.

I played on mechanically for a moment, my eyes riveted upon the grotesque antics of the insect, feeling instinctively that the music was producing this singular effect upon it. I was right; for, as I gradually paused, the gyrations of the insect assumed a milder phase, and as I ceased entirely the great, bloated thing ran far out overhead and dropped suddenly a yard below the ceiling, and, pendent by its unseen thread, hung sprawled in the empty air above my face, so near I could have touched it with the lifted instrument. And then, even as I shrank back fearfully, a new line of speculation was suggested to my mind: I arose abruptly, leaned the guitar back in the corner, took up a book, and sat down at the desk, leaving the silence of the room intensified till in my nervous state of mind I almost fancied I could hear that spider whispering to itself, as above the open pages of the book I watched the space between it and the ceiling slowly widening, till at last the ugly insect dropped and disappeared behind the sofa.

I had not long to wait; nor was my curious mind placed any more at ease, when, at last, faint and far-off sounding as at first, I heard the eerie twanging of the guitar—though this time I could with some triumphant pleasure note the fact that the instrument was in perfect tune. But to thoroughly assure myself that I could in no way be mistaken as to the mysterious cause, I arose and crept cautiously across the carpet until within easy reach of the guitar. I paused again to listen and convince myself beyond all doubt that the sounds were there produced. There could possibly be no mistake about it. Then suddenly I caught and whirled the instrument around, and as I did so the spider darted from the key-

TALE OF A SPIDER

board near the top, leaped to the broom-handle, and fled up the wall.

I tried no more experiments that night, or rather morning—for it must have been three o'clock as I turned wearily away from the exasperating contemplation of the strange subject, turned down the lamp, then turned it up again, huddled myself into a shivering heap upon the sofa, and fell into an uneasy sleep, in which I dreamed that *I* was a spider—of Brobdingnagian proportions, and lived on men and women instead of flies, and had a web like a monster hammock, in which I swung myself out over the streets at night and fished up my prey with a hook and line—thought I caught more poets than anything else, and was just nibbling warily at my own bait, when the line was suddenly withdrawn, the hook catching me in the cheek, tearing out and letting me drop back with a sullen plunge into the great gulf of the night. And as I found myself, with wildly staring eyes, sitting bolt upright on the sofa, I saw the spider, just above my desk, lifted and flung upward by his magic line and thrown among the dusky shadows of the ceiling.

"Hays," said I to my chum, in the early morning, as he came in upon me, sitting at my desk, and gazing abstractedly at an incoherent scrawl of ink upon the scrap of paper lying before me—"Hays," said I, "what's your opinion of spiders?"

"What's my opinion of spiders?" he queried, staring at me curiously.

"What's your opinion of spiders?" I repeated with my first inflection—for Hays is a young man in the medical profession, and likes point, fact, and brevity. "What I mean is this," I continued: "isn't it generally conceded that the spider is endowed with a higher order of intelligence than insects commonly?"

"I believe so," he replied, with the same curious air, watching me narrowly; "I have a vague recollection of some incident illustrative of that theory in Goldsmith's 'Animated Nature,' or some equally veracious chronicle," with suggestive emphasis on the word "veracious." "Why do you ask?" And, although half assured I would be sneered at for my pains, I went into a minute recountal of my strange experience of the night, winding up in a high state of excitement, doubtless intensified by the blandly smiling features of my auditor, who made no interruption whatever, and only looked at me at the conclusion of the dream with gratuitous compassion and concern. "Well!" said I, uneasily, taking an impatient turn or two across the room. . . . "Well!" I repeated, pausing abruptly and glaring at the shrugged shoulders of my stoical companion, "why don't you say something?"

"Nothing to say, I suppose," he answered, turning on me with absolute severity.—"You never listen to advice. Two months ago I told you to quit this night business—it would wreck you physically, mentally, every way. Why, look at you!" he continued in pitiless reproof, as I flew off on another nervous trip around the room. "Look at you! a perfect crate of bones—no 'get-up' in your walk—no color in your face—no appetite—no anything but a wisp of shattered nerves, and a pair of howling-hungry eyes that do nothing else but stare."

"It wouldn't seem that you did have much to say, upon the point, at least," I interrupted. "Never mind my physical condition; what do you think of my spider?"

"What do I think of your spider!" he repeated contemptuously; "why, I think it's a little the thinnest piece of twaddle I ever listened to!—And I think, further—"

"Hold on, now!" I exclaimed, a trifle warmed, but smiling; "I knew you'd have to sweat awhile over that: but hold on—hold on! I have only told you the minor facts of the strange occurrence; the most startling and irrefutable portion yet remains. Now, listen! What I have already told you I pledge you on my honor is pure truth. I can offer nothing but my word for that. But

TALE OF A SPIDER

I will close now—don't interrupt me, if you please: As I awakened from that dream, I saw that spider jerked from above the desk here—just as a small boy might whip up a fish-line—jerked by his own thread, of course.—Well, and I got up at once—came to the desk like this, feeling instinctively that that infernal spider had some object in lowering itself among my letters; and I found this scrap of paper, which I'll swear I left last night without one blot or line of ink or pencil on it.—I found this scrap of paper with this zigzag line—which you can see was never made with human hand—scrawled across it, and the ink was yet wet when I picked it up. *Now*, what do you say?"

He took the scrap of paper in his hand half curiously, and then, as though ashamed of having betrayed so great a weakness, threw it back upon the desk with scarce a look.

"What do you say?" I repeated, in a tone of triumph.

"Well," he replied, "it is barely possible you did see a spider in this last instance, and I must confess that it is a much easier matter for me to imagine a spider dropping by accident into your inkstand and leaving the trail of his salvation across your writing-paper, than it is for me to fancy the fantastic insect plucking the strings of your guitar. In fact, the first part of your story won't do at all. I don't mean to intimate that your veracity is defective—not at all. But I do mean that you have overworked yourself of late, and that your brain needs rest."

"But," said I, pushing the scrap of paper toward him again, "you don't seem to recognize the fact that that ugly scrawl of ink means something. Look at it carefully; it's writing."

He again took the paper in his hand, but this time without a glance, and ere I could prevent him he had torn it in a half-dozen pieces and flung it on the floor.

"What do you mean?" I cried, resentfully, springing forward.

"Why, I mean that you're a babbling idiot," he answered, in a tone half anger, half alarm; "and if you won't look after your own condition I'll do it for you, and in spite of you! You must quit this work—quit this room—quit everything, and come with me out in the fresh air for a while, or you'll die; that's what I mean!"

Although he spoke with almost savage vehemence, I recognized, of course, the real promptings of his action, and smiled softly to myself as I gathered up the scattered scraps of paper from the carpet.

"Oh, we'll not quarrel," said I, seating myself patiently at the desk, and dipping my finger in the paste-cup—

"we'll not quarrel about a little thing like this; only if you'll just wait a minute I'll show you that it does mean something.

"There!" said I, good-naturedly, when I had deftly joined the fragments in their proper places on a base of legal cap; "now you can read it; but don't tear it again, please." I think I was very white when I said that, for my companion took the paper in his hand with at least a show of interest, and looked at it long and curiously.

"Well, what is it?" he asked, laying it back upon the desk before me: "I am really very sorry, but I am forced to acknowledge that I fail to find anything exactly tangible in it."

"Look," said I; "you see this capital that begins the line; the first letter?—It's a 'Y,' isn't it?"

"Yes; it looks a little like a 'Y'—or a 'G.'"

"No; it's a 'Y,'" said I, "and there's no more doubt about it than that this next one is an 'e.'"

"Well—"

"Well, this next letter is an 'S'—an old-fashioned 'S,' but it's an 'S' all the same, and you can't make anything else out of it; I've tried it, and it can't be done."

"Well, go on."

"This is a 'c,'" I continued.

"Go on; call it anything you like."

"No; but I want you to be thoroughly satisfied."

"Oh, do you? Well, it's a 'c,' then; go on."

"And this is an 'h.'"

"Go on."

"And this is an 'o'; you know that!"

"Yes; know it by the hole in it."

"Don't get funny. And this is an 'l.'"

"That's an 'l.'"

"This is an 'a.'"

"Close observer!"

"And that's an 'r'—and that's all."

"Well, you've got it all down to suit you; now, what does it spell?"

"What does it spell? Why, can't you read?" I exclaimed, flourishing the scrap triumphantly before his eyes. "It spells 'Ye Scholar!'—why, I could read it across the room!"

"Yes, or across the street," he answered, caustically. "But come now!" he continued, seriously, "throw it aside for the present at least, and let's go out in the sunshine for a while. Here, light a cigar, and come along"; and he moved toward the door.

"No," said I, turning to the mysterious scrawl, "I shall hound this thing down while the inspiration's on me."

TALE OF A SPIDER

"Inspiration?—Bah!" The door slammed, but I never turned my head.

I had sat thus in dead silence for ten minutes, when suddenly I heard a quick, impatient movement at my back, and then the sharp, impetuous words—"In God's name! quit biting your nails like that! Don't you know it's an indication of madness!"

I think I need not enter into any explanation as to the reason which, from that moment, determined me upon a course that could afford no further conflict of opinion other than that already going on within my own mind. That of itself furnished all exasperating controversy that I felt was well for my indulgence. But in one sense I was grateful for the pointed suggestion of my friend regarding the questionable status of my mental faculties, for by it I was made most keenly alive to that peculiar sense of duty that made me look upon myself and question every individual act, entirely separated from my own personality; in fact, to look upon myself, as I did, clearly and distinctly defined in the light of a very suspicious and a very dangerous character, whose sole intent and purpose was to play and practise upon me all unlooked-for and undreamed-of deceptions, and which, to successfully combat, must needs require the most rigid and unwavering strength of reason.

TALE OF A SPIDER

In further justice to my honesty in this resolve, I will say that I at once began the exercise of systematic habits. Although by no means pleasant, I took long rambles in the country; ate regularly of wholesome food, regained my appetite, and retired at night at seasonable hours. I will not say that sleep came sooner to my eyes by reason of the change, but I wooed sleep, anyway—let this suffice. I threw smoking entirely aside —not a hard trial for me by any means, although an occasional cigar is a great pleasure; but I threw it aside. Did not study so intensely as had been my wont; read but little, and wrote less—even neglecting my letters. Yet, with all this revolution of reform, I am left to confess that I never for one waking moment forgot the mystic legend, "Ye Scholar," or its equally incomprehensible author; and how could I?

Since the first discovery of the strange insect and its musical proclivities, but three evenings only have passed that I have not been favored with its most extraordinary performances on the guitar. In this way has its presence been usually made known. And noting carefully, as I have done, the peculiar times and conditions of its coming, together with such other suggestions as the surroundings have afforded me, I have been led to believe that the spider reasoned as a man would reason: In no instance

TALE OF A SPIDER

yet has it ever touched the instrument when I sat busy at my desk; and only when my pen was idle in my hand, or I had turned wearily away to pace about the room, has it ever exhibited any inclination whatever to occupy my attention. This curious fact interpreted itself at last in the rather startling proposition that it was simply an indication on the part of the insect that it desired me to favor it with music, since my time was not better occupied.—Virtually this is what it *did* mean; I *know* it! I would know and appreciate now any want the insect might choose to express; only at first I was very dull, as one would be naturally. And I noticed, too, that when I first responded to this summons the spider would leap from the guitar to the wall with every evidence of pleasure, and glide back to its old position near the ceiling, indulging the wildest tokens of glee and approval throughout my performances. And many times I have marched off round and round the room simply thrumming the time, the spider following along the upper margin of the wall with the most fantastic caperings of joy.

Other experiments followed, too numerous and too foolish for recountal here, but each, in its way, sufficient to more conclusively establish in my mind the belief that the hideous little monster was endowed with an intelligence as wise and subtle in its workings as was within the power of my own to recognize—even greater, —for gradually, as we became more accustomed to each other, the ugly insect grew so tame it would come down the wall and dance for me on a level with my face as I sat playing, and even spring off upon the instrument if I held it out. I found my mind so baffled and bewildered at last that more than once the conviction has been forced upon me that the spider was *not* a spider, but a— No, I'll not say that—not yet, not yet!

These experiments had progressed for perhaps half a dozen nights, when, one evening, as I sat, pen in hand, at the desk here, mechanically poring over the still incomprehensible meaning of the scrawl, and writing and rewriting the two words over and over again upon an empty page before me, I became suddenly aware of a strange sensation of repose. A great, cool quiet fell upon my brain, as when suddenly within some noisy foundry the clanging hammers cease to beat and all the brazen tumult drops like a plummet into silence fathomless. I felt a soothing languor flowing down and over me, and ebbing through and through my very being. It was not drowsiness; my eyelids were not heavy, nor did they droop the shadow of a shade. I saw everything about me as clearly as I do this very moment—only, I did not seem a part of my surroundings. My eyes, although conscious of all objects within range, were fixed upon the scrap of paper headed by the zigzag scrawl, and with an intensity of gaze that seemed to pierce the paper and to see through it and beyond it; and I did not think it strange. I was dimly conscious, too, of being under the control of some hitherto undreamed-of influence, but I felt no thought of resistance—rather courted the sensation. All was utter calm with me; and I did not think it strange. I saw my hand held out before me in this same position—the forearm resting on the desk—the same pen grasped lightly in my fingers. Slowly—slowly—slowly—I saw the spider lowering itself above it, wavering and swaying in the air, until, at last, I saw it reach its dangling legs and clutch and cling to the penholder at the tip, and rest there; and I did not think it strange. But I grew duller then, and very chilly, though I vividly recall seeing the hand moved—not of my own volition—the pen dipped in the ink, and brought directly over the old scrap whereon the scrawl was traced; and I remember, too, that as I watched the motion of my hand, I still saw beyond the surface of the paper, and read the very words my pen traced afterward. I say the words my pen traced—or my hand—either—both,—for the act was not my own, I swear! And the spider still sat

TALE OF A SPIDER

perched there at his post, rocked lightly with the motion of the pen, with all his arms hugged round him as though chuckling to himself; and I say to you again, and yet again, I did not think it strange.

Not until the page before me had been filled did I regain my natural state of being, nor did it seem that I then would, had not the spider quitted his position and ran down the penholder, leaning from it for an instant, touching and pressing my naked hand: then I was conscious of a keen, exquisite sting; and with a quick, spasmodic motion I flung the hideous insect from it. As I lifted my white face and starting eyes, I saw the spider wildly clambering toward the ceiling on its invisible thread; and then, with a mingled sense of fear, bewilderment, and admiration, as oppressive and as strange as indescribable, I turned to the mysterious scrap and read, traced tremblingly, but plainly, in a dainty, flowing hand, unlike any I had ever seen before, the lines I now copy from the original script before me, bearing the pedantic title of "Ye Scholar":

> "Ho! ho! Ye Scholar recketh not how lean
>   His lank frame waxeth in ye hectic gloom
>   That smeareth o'er ye dim walls of his room
> His wavering shadow! Shut is he, I ween,
> Like as a withered nosegay, in between

TALE OF A SPIDER

> Ye musty, mildewed leaves of some volume
> Of ancient lore ye moth and he consume
> In jointure. Yet a something in his mien
> Forbids all mockery, though quaint is he,
> And eke fantastical in form and face
> As that Old Knight ye Tale of Chivalry
> Made mad immortally, yet spared ye grace
> Of some rare virtue which we sigh to see,
> And pour our laughter out most tenderly."

Over and over I read the strange production to myself; and, as at last I started to my feet repeating it aloud, all suddenly the spider swooped on its flying thread before my upturned face, swung back upon the margin of the wall, and went scampering round and round above me as I read.

I did not sleep two hours of the night, but mouthed and mouthed that sonnet—even in my scrappy dreams—until when morning strained the sunlight through the slatted window-blinds, I turned and dragged myself from the room like an old, old man with childish summer fancies in his head and bleak and barren winter in his bones.

The night following, and the next night, and the next, I did not permit myself to enter my room after dark—not from a sense of fear, but simply because I felt my mind

TALE OF A SPIDER

was becoming too entirely engrossed with the contemplation of a theme that, even yet at times, I feared was more chimera than reality. Throughout the day I worked, as usual with me, perhaps three hours, at such trivial tasks as required only the lightest mental effort; nor did I allow my mind to wander from the matter-of-fact duties before me to the contemplation of the ever-present topic that so confounded it when studiously dwelt upon. Only once in this long abstinence from the fascinating problem did I catch sight of the spider, peering down upon me from behind the shoulder of the little terra-cotta bust of Dickens that sits on a dusty bracket just above my desk. I looked up at the little fellow with a smile, rose to my feet, and held out my hand, when, at the motion, the insect cowered trembling for an instant, then sprang up the wall beyond my reach. But from that time on I always felt its presence though unseen, intuitively conscious that at all hours my every act was vigilantly overlooked and guarded by the all-seeing eye of that spider, and that every motion of my pen was duly noted by it, and accepted as token of the fact that I was busy and must not be disturbed. In fact, I even allowed my vanity such license that I came to believe that the spider was not only interested in everything I did, but was actually proud of my accomplishments besides. Certain it is, I argued, that he likes my silence, my music, and my voice, and equally apparent from his actions that he likes my society under any and all circumstances, and it shall not be the promptings of mere curiosity on my part in the endeavor to strengthen and develop this curious bond of fellowship, but my serious and most courteous duty as well.

So I went back to my night labors, even greeted, the first evening, as I lit my lamp and sat down at the desk, with another mysterious scrawl, which I readily interpreted in the one word "Love."

I dashed the scrap down in a very spasm of revulsion and loathing. I cannot describe nor will I weaken the sense of utter abhorrence that fell upon me by an attempt to set it forth in words; why, I could taste it, and it sickened me soul-deep! I remember catching quick breaths through my clinched and naked teeth; I remember snatching up the pen as a despairing man might grasp a dagger; I remember stabbing it in the ink, and drawing it back in defiance; but as my hand once more rested on the desk it was my hand no longer.—It was like another man's, and that man my deadly foe. I looked upon it vengefully, wishing that in my other I but held an axe—an old axe, with a nicked and rusty edge,—

that I might hack and haggle the traitor-member sheer off at the numb and pulseless wrist. And then the spider! I tried to shrink back as the hideous insect again dangled before my eyes, but could not move. Once more it clutched the holder of the pen, huddled its quivering limbs together, and squatted in its old position on the tip. And then began the movement of the hand.

This time my eyes were fixed upon the insect. I could not move them from it. I could see nothing else; and but for the undulating motions of the pen I felt that I might note its very breathings—and I *did* see it *smile*. Oh, horrible! Why, I set my teeth together till my inner sense of hearing pinged like a bell, and I said, away down among the twanging fibres of my heart, "I will kill you for that smile! I will kill you—kill you!" And when at last the motion of the hand had ceased, and the hideous insect again ran down the penholder, leaning, and pressing into my naked flesh that keen, exquisite sting, I snapped the thrall that bound me, flung the spider violently against the desk, stabbed the pen wildly at it with a dozen swift, vindictive motions as the abhorrent thing lay for the moment writhing on its back. And I struck it, too, and pinioned it; but as for an instant I turned away from the revolting sight, my pen still quivering above it, sunken eye-deep in the desk, my victim yet escaped me, for, as I turned again, no sign remained to designate my murderous deed but one poor severed limb, twitching and trembling in ever-lessening throes and convulsions.

I turned my eyes upon the mysterious scrap once more, with the same unaccountable feeling of dread and revulsion that had possessed me as I read the scrawl. Written in the same minute, tremulous but legible hand in which the first was traced, I read:

> "O, what strange tragedy is this of mine
>   That wars within, and will not let me cry?
>   My soul seems leaking from me sigh by sigh;
> And yet I dare not say—nor he divine—
> That I, so vile and loathsome in design,
>   Am brimmed with boiling love; but I must lie
>   Forever steeped in seething agony!
> If all these quivering arms might wreathe and twine,
>   And soak him up in one warm clasp of bliss—
> One long caress, when babbling wild with words
>   My voice were crushed and mangled with his kiss,—
> My soul would whistle sweeter than the birds.—
>   But now, my dry and husky heart in this
>   Pent heat of gasping passion can but hiss!"

Be patient! I am hurrying toward the end. I am very lonesome here alone. For three long, empty nights have

TALE OF A SPIDER

I sat thus, with nothing but the raspings of my pen for company. I cannot sleep now; and I wouldn't if I could. My head feels as if I had a very heavy hat on, and I put up my hand sometimes to see. My head is feverish, that's all. I have been working too late again. Last night I heard Hays come up the steps—my window opens on an alley, but at night the light shows from the street. Hays has a peculiar walk: I'd know it if I heard it in the grass above my grave. And he came up the stairs last night, and knocked and rattled at the door; but I was very still, and so he went away. Sometimes I think that fellow isn't right exactly in his mind. I never knew what silence was before. It will not even whisper to me now. Sometimes I stop and listen, and then it holds its breath and listens too—but we never hear a thing. The old guitar leans in the corner with its face turned to the wall. I know it's sorry, but it would be such a comfort to me if it would only moan or murmur as it used to. I always tune it the first thing when I come in, and lean it back, just as it was when the spider first began to play it; but the spider won't go near it any more. Even the spider has deserted me, and gone away and left me here alone—all alone! One night, late, I heard it coming up the stairs; and it knocked and rattled at the door, and I wouldn't let it in, and so it went away—and do you know

TALE OF A SPIDER

that I have often thought that that spider wasn't right —in its mind, you know? Oh, yes! I have often thought so—often! This hat bothers me, but I'll hurry on—I must hurry on.

When I came in to-night—no; *last* night it was— when I came to work last night, there was another of those scrawls the spider had left for me, and it was written in a very trembling hand. The letters were blotted and slurred together so I could hardly make the word out; but I did make it out, and it was simply the one word, "Death"—just "Death." I didn't like the looks of it, and I tried to make it read something else; but it wouldn't. It was "Death." And so I laid it gently on the desk and walked about the room very softly for a long time. And the night kept on getting stiller, and stiller, and stiller, till it just stopped. But that didn't disturb me; I was not sleepy, anyhow, and so I sat down at the desk, took up my pen, and waited. I had nothing else to do, and the guitar wouldn't play any more, and I was lonesome; so I sat down at the desk, and took up the pen, and waited.

Sometimes I think it's those spells the spider gives me that make my head feel this way. It feels like I had a heavy hat on; but I haven't any hat on at all, and if I had

TALE OF A SPIDER

I wouldn't have it on here in the room. I can't even sit in the cars with a hat on.

And so I waited, and waited; but it seemed like it hadn't got still enough for the spider yet. It was still enough for me; but I got to thinking about why the spider didn't come, and concluded at last that it wasn't still enough yet for the spider. So I waited till it got so still I could see it: and then the spider came sliding along down through it; and when it touched the penholder, and I got a good clear look at it, I flashed dead-numb clean to the marrow.—It was so pale! Did you ever see a spider after it has had a long spell of sickness? That's the way this spider looked. I shuddered as it huddled its trembling legs together and sat down. And then the pen moved off, with that pale, ghastly, haggard insect nodding away again as though it still were victor of the field; and as, at last, I found courage to peer closer into its face, I saw that same accursed smile flung back at me. All pity and compassion fled away, and I felt my heart snarl rabidly and champ its bloody jaws with deadly hate. And when the spider hobbled down the penholder and touched my hand again, the only sting I felt upon it was the vengeful blow I smote it with the other, as I held and ground it there with an exultant cry that rang out upon the silence till the echoes clapped their very hands and shouted with me, "Dead! dead at last! Dead! dead! and I am free!" Oh, how I revelled in my fancied triumph as I danced about the room, crunching my hands together till I thought that I could feel the clammy fragments of the hateful thing gaumed and slimed about between my palms and fingers! And what a fool I was! for when at last I unclasped them and spread them wide apart in utter loathing, they were as free from taint or moisture as they are this very moment; and then it all flashed on me that I was in some horrid dream—some hideous, baleful nightmare—some fell delusion of a fevered sleep. But no! I could not force that comfort on myself, for here the lamp sat burning brightly as at this very moment, and I reached and held my finger on the chimney till it burned. I wheeled across the room, opened the door, went to the window and raised it, and felt the chill draught sweeping in upon my fevered face. I took my hat from the sofa and dashed out into the night. I was not asleep; I had not been asleep; for not until broad daylight did I return, to find the window opened just as I had left it; the lamp still blazing at its fullest glare, and that grim scrawl, "Death," lying still upon the desk, with these lines traced legibly beneath it:

TALE OF A SPIDER

"And did you know our old friend Death is dead?
  Ah me! he died last night; my ghost was there,
  And all his phantom-friends from everywhere
Were sorrowfully grouped about his bed.
'I die; God help the living now!' he said
  With such a ghastly pathos, I declare
  The tears oozed from the blind eyes of the air
And spattered on his face in gouts of red.
And then he smiled—the dear old bony smile
  That glittered on us in that crazy whim
When first our daring feet leapt the defile
  Of life and ran so eagerly to him:
And so he smiled upon us, even while
  The kind old sockets grew forever dim."

I am almost through. It is nearly morning as I write. When daylight comes, and this is finished, I can sleep.

That last spider that appeared to me was not the real spider. That last spider was not a spider, and I'll tell you how I know: Four hours ago, as I sat writing here, I dipped and dragged a strange clot from the inkstand with my pen. It is barely dry yet, and it is a drowned spider. It is the real spider—the other spider was its ghost. Listen: I know this is the real spider from the fact that it has one leg missing, and the leg that has been lying on my desk here, for three days and nights, I find, upon careful examination and adjustment, is the leg that originally supplied this deficiency.

Whatever theory it may please you to advance regarding the mysterious manifestations of the spider while in the flesh will doubtless be as near the correct one as my own. Certainly I shall not attempt to controvert any opinion you may choose to express. I simply reserve the right, in conclusion of my story, to say that I believe this spider met his death by suicide.

WHERE IS MARY ALICE SMITH?

WHERE IS MARY ALICE SMITH?

"WHERE—is—Mary—Alice—Smith? Oh—she—has—gone—home!" It was the thin, mysterious voice of little Mary Alice Smith herself that so often queried and responded as above—every word accented with a sweet and eerie intonation, and a very gayety of solemn earnestness that baffled the cunning skill of all childish imitators. A slender wisp of a girl she was, not more than ten years of age in appearance, though it had been given to us as fourteen. The spindle ankles that she so airily flourished from the sparse concealment of a worn and shadowy calico skirt seemed scarce a fraction more in girth than the slim, blue-veined wrists she tossed among the loose and ragged tresses of her yellow hair, as she danced around the room. She was, from the first, an object of curious and most refreshing interest to our family—to us children in particular—an interest, though years and years have interposed to shroud it in the dull

WHERE IS MARY ALICE SMITH?

dust of forgetfulness, that still remains vivid and bright and beautiful. Whether an orphan child only, or with a father that could thus lightly send her adrift, I do not know now, nor do I care to ask, but I do recall distinctly that on a raw, bleak day in early winter she was brought to us, from a wild country settlement, by a reputed uncle —a gaunt, round-shouldered man, with deep eyes and sallow cheeks and weedy-looking beard, as we curiously watched him from the front window stolidly swinging this little, blue-lipped, red-nosed waif over the muddy wagon-wheel to father's arms, like so much country produce. And even as the man resumed his seat upon the thick board laid across the wagon, and sat chewing a straw, with spasmodic noddings of the head, as some brief further conference detained him, I remember mother quickly lifting my sister up from where we stood, folding and holding the little form in unconscious counterpart of father and the little girl without. And how we gathered round her when father brought her in, and mother fixed a cosey chair for her close to the blazing fire, and untied the little summer hat, with its hectic trimmings, together with the dismal green veil that had been bound beneath it round the little, tingling ears. The hollow, pale-blue eyes of the child followed every motion with an alertness that suggested a somewhat suspicious mind.

WHERE IS MARY ALICE SMITH?

"Dave gimme that!" she said, her eyes proudly following the hat as mother laid it on the pillow of the bed. "Mustn't git it mussed up, sir! er you'll have Dave in yer wool!" she continued, warningly, as our childish interest drew us to a nearer view of the gaudy article in question.

Half awed, we shrank back to our first wonderment, one of us, however, with the bravery to ask: "Who's Dave?"

"Who's Dave?" reiterated the little voice, half scornfully.—"W'y, Dave's a great big boy! Dave works on Barnes's place. And he kin purt'-nigh make a full hand, too. Dave's purt'-nigh tall as your pap! He's purt'-nigh growed up—Dave is! And—David—Mason—Jeffries," she continued, jauntily teetering her head from left to right, and for the first time introducing that peculiar deliberation of accent and undulating utterance that we afterward found to be her quaintest and most charming characteristic—" and— David— Mason —Jeffries —he— likes—Mary—Alice—Smith!" And then she broke abruptly into the merriest laughter, and clapped her little palms together till they fairly glowed.

"And who's Mary Alice Smith?" clamored a chorus of merry voices.

The elfish figure straightened haughtily in the chair.

WHERE IS MARY ALICE SMITH?

Folding the slender arms tightly across her breast, and tilting her wan face back with an imperious air, she exclaimed sententiously, "W'y, Mary Alice Smith is me—that's who Mary Alice Smith is!"

It was not long, however, before her usual bright and infectious humor was restored, and we were soon piloting the little stranger here and there about the house, and laughing at the thousand funny things she said and did. The winding stairway in the hall quite dazed her with delight. Up and down she went a hundred times, it seemed. And she would talk and whisper to herself, and oftentimes would stop and nestle down and rest her pleased face close against a step and pat it softly with her slender hand, peering curiously down at us with half-averted eyes. And she counted them and named them, every one, as she went up and down.

"I'm mighty glad I'm come to live in this-here house," she said.

We asked her why.

"Oh, 'cause," she said, starting up the stairs again by an entirely novel and original method of her own—"'cause Uncle Tomps ner Aunt 'Lizabeth don't live here; and when they ever come here to git their dinners, like they will ef you don't watch out, w'y, then I kin slip out here on these-here stairs and play like I was climbin'

WHERE IS MARY ALICE SMITH?

up to the Good World where my mother is—that's why!"

Then we hushed our laughter, and asked her where her home was, and what it was like, and why she didn't like her Uncle Tomps and Aunt 'Lizabeth, and if she wouldn't want to visit them sometimes.

"Oh, yes," she artlessly answered in reply to the concluding query; "I'll want to go back there lots o' times; but not to see them! I'll—only—go—back—there—to—see"—and here she was holding up the little flared-out fingers of her left hand, and with the index-finger of the right touching their pink tips in ordered notation with the accent of every gleeful word—"I'll —only— go —back —there —to—see—David—Mason—Jeffries—'cause—he's—the—boy—fer—me!" And then she clapped her hands again and laughed in that half-hysterical, half-musical way of hers till we all joined in and made the echoes of the old hall ring again. "And then," she went on, suddenly throwing out an imperative gesture of silence—"and then, after I've been in this-here house a long, long time, and you all git so's you like me awful—awful—awful well, then some day you'll go in that room there—and that room there—and in the kitchen—and out on the porch—and down the cellar—and out in the smoke-house—and the wood-house—and the loft—and all around—Oh, ever' place—and in here—and up the stairs—and all them rooms up there—and you'll look behind all the doors—and in all the cubboards—and under all the beds—and then you'll look sorry-like, and holler out, kindo' skeert, and you'll say: 'Where—is—Mary—Alice—Smith?' And then you'll wait and listen and hold yer breath; and then somepin'll holler back, away fur off, and say: 'Oh—she—has—gone—home!' And then ever'thing'll be all still ag'in, and you'll be afeard to holler any more—and you dursn't play—and you can't laugh, and yer throat'll thist hurt and hurt, like you been a-eatin' too much calamus-root er somepin'!" And as the little gypsy concluded her weird prophecy, with a final flourish of her big, pale eyes, we glanced furtively at one another's awe-struck faces, with a superstitious dread of a vague, indefinite disaster most certainly awaiting us around some shadowy corner of the future. Through all this speech she had been slowly and silently groping up the winding steps, her voice growing fainter and fainter, and the little pixy-form fading, and wholly vanishing at last around the spiral banister of the upper landing. Then down to us from that alien recess came the voice alone, touched with a tone as of wild entreaty and despair: "Where—is—Mary—Alice—Smith?" And then a long, breathless pause,

WHERE IS MARY ALICE SMITH?

in which our wide-eyed group below huddled still closer, pale and mute. Then—far off and faint and quavering with a tenderness of pathos that dews the eyes of memory even now—came, like a belated echo, the voice all desolate: "Oh—she—has—gone—home!"

What a queer girl she was, and what a fascinating influence she unconsciously exerted over us! We never tired of her presence; but she, deprived of ours by the many household tasks that she herself assumed, so rigidly maintained and deftly executed, seemed always just as happy when alone as when in our boisterous, fun-loving company. Such resources had Mary Alice Smith—such a wonderfully inventive fancy! She could talk to herself—a favorite amusement, I might almost say a popular amusement, of hers, since these monologues at times would involve numberless characters, chipping in from manifold quarters of a wholesale discussion, and querying and exaggerating, agreeing and controverting, till the dishes she was washing would clash and clang excitedly in the general badinage. Loaded with a pyramid of glistening cups and saucers, she would improvise a gallant line of march from the kitchen table to the pantry, heading an imaginary procession, and whistling a fife-tune that would stir your blood. Then she would trippingly return, rippling her rosy fingers up and down the

WHERE IS MARY ALICE SMITH?

keys of an imaginary portable piano, or stammering flat-soled across the floor, chuffing and tooting like a locomotive. And she would gravely propound to herself the most intricate riddles—ponder thoughtfully and in silence over them—hazard the most ridiculous answers, and laugh derisively at her own affected ignorance. She would guess again and again, and assume the most gleeful surprise upon at last giving the proper answer, and then she would laugh jubilantly, and mockingly scout herself with having given out "a fool-riddle" that she could guess "with both eyes shut."

"Talk about riddles," she said abruptly to us, one evening after supper, as we lingered watching her clearing away the table—"talk about riddles, it—takes—David—Mason—Jeffries—to—tell—riddles! Bet you don't know

> 'Riddle-cum, riddle-cum right!
> Where was I last Saturd'y night?
> The winds did blow—the boughs did shake—
> I saw the hole a fox did make!'"

Again we felt that indefinable thrill never separate from the strange utterance, suggestive always of some dark mystery, and fascinating and holding the childish fancy in complete control.

WHERE IS MARY ALICE SMITH?

"Bet you don't know this-'un neether:

    'A holler-hearted father,
      And a hump-back mother—
    Three black orphants
      All born together!'"

We were dumb.

"You can't guess nothin'!" she said, half pityingly. "W'y, them's easy as fallin' off a chunk! First-'un's a man named Fox, and he kilt his wife and chopped her head off, and they was a man named Wright lived in that neighberhood—and he was a-goin' home—and it was Saturd'y night—and he was a-comin' through the big woods—and they was a storm—and Wright he clumb a tree to git out the rain, and while he was up there here come along a man with a dead woman—and a pickaxe, and a spade. And he drug the dead woman under the same tree where Mr. Wright was—so ever' time it 'ud lightnin', w'y, Wright he could look down and see him a-diggin' a grave there to bury the woman in. So Wright he kep' still tel he got her buried all right, you know, and went back home; and then he clumb down and lit out fer town, and waked up the constabul—and he got a supeeny and went out to Fox's place, and had him jerked up 'fore the gran' jury. Then, when

WHERE IS MARY ALICE SMITH?

Fox was in court and wanted to know where their proof was that he kilt his wife, w'y, Wright he jumps up and says that riddle to the judge and all the neighbers that was there. And so when they got it all studied out—w'y, they tuk old Fox out and hung him under the same tree where he buried Mrs. Fox under. And that's all o' that'n; and the other'n—I promised—David—Mason—Jeffries—I wouldn't—never—tell—no—livin'—soul—'less—he—gimme—leef,—er—they—guessed—it—out—their—own—se'f!" And as she gave this rather ambiguous explanation of the first riddle, with the mysterious comment on the latter in conclusion, she shook her elfin tresses back over her shoulders with a cunning toss of her head and a glimmering twinkle of her pale, bright eyes that somehow reminded us of the fairy godmother in Cinderella.

And Mary Alice Smith was right, too, in her early prognostications regarding the visits of her Uncle Tomps and Aunt 'Lizabeth. Many times through the winter they "jest dropped in," as Aunt 'Lizabeth always expressed it, "to see how we was a-gittin' on with Mary Alice." And once, "in court week," during a prolonged trial in which Uncle Tomps and Aunt 'Lizabeth rather prominently figured, they "jest dropped in" upon us and settled down and dwelt with us for the longest five days and nights we children had ever in our lives experienced. Nor was our long term of restraint from childish sports relieved wholly by their absence, since Aunt 'Lizabeth had taken Mary Alice back with them, saying that "a good long visit to her dear old home—pore as it was—would do the child good."

And then it was that we went about the house in moody silence, the question, "Where—is—Mary—Alice—Smith?" forever yearning at our lips for utterance, and the still belated echo in the old hall overhead forever answering, "Oh—she—has—gone—home!"

It was early spring when she returned. And we were looking for her coming, and knew a week beforehand the very day she would arrive—for had not Aunt 'Lizabeth sent special word by Uncle Tomps, who "had come to town to do his millin', and git the latest war news, not to fail to jest drop in and tell us that they was layin' off to send Mary Alice in next Saturd'y."

Our little town, like every other village and metropolis throughout the country at that time, was, to the children at least, a scene of continuous holiday and carnival. The nation's heart was palpitating with the feverish pulse of war, and already the still half-frozen clods of the common highway were beaten into frosty dust by the tread of marshalled men; and the shrill shriek of the fife, and the hoarse boom and jar and rattling patter of the drums stirred every breast with something of that rapturous insanity of which true patriots and heroes can alone be made.

But on that day—when Mary Alice Smith was to return—what was all the gallant tumult of the town to us? I remember how we ran far up the street to welcome her—for afar off we had recognized her elfish face and eager eyes peering expectantly from behind the broad shoulders of a handsome fellow mounted on a great high-stepping horse that neighed and pranced excitedly as we ran skurrying toward them.

"Whoo-ee!" she cried, in perfect ecstasy, as we paused in breathless admiration. "Clear—the—track—there, —old—folks—young—folks!—fer—Mary—Alice—Smith—and—David—Mason—Jeffries—is—come—to—town!"

O what a day that was! And how vain indeed would be the attempt to detail here a tithe of its glory, or our happiness in having back with us our dear little girl, and her hysterical delight in seeing us so warmly welcome to the full love of our childish hearts the great, strong, round-faced, simple-natured "David—Mason—Jeffries"! Long and long ago we had learned to love him as we loved the peasant hero of some fairy tale of Christian

Andersen's; but now that he was with us in most wholesome and robust verity, our very souls seemed scampering from our bodies to run to him and be caught up and tossed and swung and dandled in his gentle, giant arms.

All that long delicious morning we were with him. In his tender charge we were permitted to go down among the tumult and the music of the streets, his round, good-humored face and big blue eyes lit with a lustre like our own. And happy little Mary Alice Smith — how proud she was of him! And how closely and how tenderly, through all that golden morning, did the strong brown hand clasp hers! A hundred times at least, as we promenaded thus, she swung her head back jauntily to whisper to us in that old mysterious way of hers that " David — Mason — Jeffries — and — Mary — Alice — Smith — knew — something — that — we — couldn't — guess!" But when he had returned us home, and after dinner had started down the street alone, with little Mary Alice clapping her hands after him above the gate and laughing in a strange new voice, and with the backs of her little, fluttering hands vainly striving to blot out the big tear-drops that gathered in her eyes, we vaguely guessed the secret she and David kept. That night at suppertime we knew it fully. He had enlisted.

. . . .

WHERE IS MARY ALICE SMITH?

Among the list of "killed" at Rich Mountain, Va., occurred the name of "Jeffries, David M." We kept it from her while we could. At last she knew.

. . . . . .

"It don't seem like no year ago to me!" Over and over she had said these words. The face was very pale and thin, and the eyes so bright—so bright! The kindly hand that smoothed away the little sufferer's hair trembled and dropped tenderly again upon the folded ones beneath the snowy spread.

"Git me out the picture again!"

The trembling hand lifted once more and searched beneath the pillow.

She drew the thin hands up, and, smiling, pressed the pictured face against her lips. "David—Mason—Jeffries," she said—"le's—me—and—you—go—play—out—on—the—stairs!"

And ever in the empty home a voice goes moaning on and on, and "Where is Mary Alice Smith?" it cries, and "Where—is—Mary—Alice—Smith?" And the still belated echo, through the high depths of the old hall overhead, answers quaveringly back, "Oh—she—has—gone—home!" But her voice—it is silent evermore!

"Oh, Where is Mary Alice Smith?" She taught us how to call her thus—and now she will not answer us! Have we no voice to reach her with? How sweet and pure and glad they were in those old days, as we recall the accents ringing through the hall—the same we vainly cry to her. Her fancies were so quaint—her ways so full of prankish mysteries! We laughed then; now, upon our knees, we wring our lifted hands and gaze, through streaming tears, high up the stair she used to climb in childish glee, to call and answer eerily. And now, no answer anywhere!

How deft the little finger-tips in every task! The hands, how smooth and delicate to lull and soothe! And the strange music of her lips! The very crudeness of their speech made chaster yet the childish thought her guileless utterance had caught from spirit-depths beyond our reach. And so her homely name grew fair and sweet and beautiful to hear, blent with the echoes pealing clear and vibrant up the winding stair: "Where—where is Mary Alice Smith?" She taught us how to call her thus—but oh, she will not answer us! We have no voice to reach her with.

ECCENTRIC MR. CLARK

ECCENTRIC MR. CLARK

ALL who knew Mr. Clark intimately, casually, or by sight alone, smiled always, meeting him, and thought, "What an odd man he is!" Not that there was anything extremely or ridiculously obtrusive in Mr. Clark's peculiarities, either of feature, dress, or deportment, by which a graded estimate of his really quaint character might be aptly defined; but rather, perhaps, it was the curious combination of all these things that had gained for Mr. Clark the transient celebrity of being a very eccentric man.

And Mr. Clark, of all the odd inhabitants of the busy metropolis in which he lived, seemed least conscious of the fact of his local prominence. True it was that when familiarly addressed as "Clark, old boy," by sportive individuals he never recollected having seen before, he would oftentimes stare blankly in return, and with evident embarrassment; but as these actions may have been attributable to weak eyes, or to the confusion consequent upon being publicly recognized by the quondam associates of bacchanalian hours, the suggestive facts only served to throw his eccentricities in new relief.

And, in the minds of many, that Mr. Clark was somewhat given to dissipation, there was but little doubt; for, although in no way, and at no time, derelict in the rigid duties imposed upon him as an accountant in a wholesale liquor house on South John Street, a grand majority of friends had long ago conceded that a certain puffiness of flesh and a soiled-like pallor of complexion were in no wise the legitimate result of over-application simply in the counting-room of the establishment in which he found employment; but as to the complicity of Mr. Clark's direct associates in this belief, it is only justice to the gentleman to state that by them he was exonerated beyond all such suspicion, from the gray-haired senior of the firm, down to the pink-nosed porter of the warerooms, who, upon every available occasion, would point out the eccentric Mr. Clark as "the on'y man in the biznez 'at never sunk a 'thief' er drunk a drop o' 'goods' o' any kind, under no consideration!"

And Mr. Clark himself, when playfully approached upon the subject, would quietly assert that never, under any circumstances, had the taste of intoxicating liquors passed his lips, though at such asseverations it was a noticeable fact that Mr. Clark's complexion invariably grew more sultry than its wont, and that his eyes, forever moist, grew dewier, and that his lips and tongue would seem covertly entering upon some lush conspiracy, which in its incipiency he would be forced to smother with his hastily drawn handkerchief. Then the eccentric Mr. Clark would laugh nervously, and, pouncing on some subject so vividly unlike the one just previous as to daze the listener, he would ripple ahead with a tide of eloquence that positively overflowed and washed away all remembrance of the opening topic.

In point of age Mr. Clark might have been thirty, thirty-five, or even forty years, were one to venture an opinion solely guided by outward appearances and under certain circumstances and surroundings. As, for example, when, a dozen years ago, the writer of this sketch rode twenty miles in a freight-caboose with Mr. Clark as the only other passenger, he seemed in age at first not less than thirty-five; but upon opening a conversation with him, in which he joined with wonderful vivacity, a nearer view, and a prolonged and studious one as well, revealed the rather curious fact that, at the very limit of all allowable supposition, his age could not possibly have exceeded twenty-five. What it was in the man that struck me as eccentric at that time I have never been wholly able to define, but I recall accurately the most trivial occurrences of our meeting and the very subject-matter of our conversation. I even remember the very words in which he declined a drink from my travelling-flask—for "It's a raw day," I said, by way of gratuitous excuse for offering it. "Yes," he said, smilingly motioning the temptation aside; "it is a raw day; but you're rather young in years to be doctoring the weather—at least you'd better change the treatment—they'll all be raw days for you after a while!" I confess that I even felt an inward pity for the man as I laughingly drained his health and returned the flask to my valise. But when I asked him, ten minutes later, the nature of the business in which he was engaged, and he handed me, in response and without comment, the card of a wholesale liquor house, with his own name in crimson letters struck diagonally across the surface, I winked naïvely to myself and thought "Ah-ha!" And, as if reading my very musings, he said: "Why, certainly, I carry a full line of samples; but, my dear young friend, don't imagine for a minute that I refuse your brand on that account. You can rest assured that I have nothing better in my cases. Whiskey is whiskey wherever it is found, and there is no 'best' whiskey—not in all the world!"

Truly, I thought, this is an odd source for the emanation of temperance sentiments—then said aloud: "And yet you engage in a business you dislike! Traffic in an article that you yourself condemn! Do I understand you?"

"Might there not be such a thing," he said, quietly, "as inheriting a business—the same as inheriting an appetite? However, one advances by gradations: I shall *sell* no more. This is my last trip on the road in that capacity: I am coming in now to take charge of the firm's books. Would be glad to have you call on me any time you're in the city. Good-bye." And, as he swung off the slowly moving train, now entering the city, and I stood watching him from the open door of the caboose as he rapidly walked down a suburban street, I was positive his gait was anything but steady—that the step—the figure—the whole air of the man was that of one then laboring under the effects of partial intoxication.

I have always liked peculiar people; no matter where I met them, no matter who they were; if once impressed with an eccentricity of character which I have reason to believe purely unaffected, I never quite forget the person, name or place of our first meeting, or where the interesting party may be found again. And so it was in the customary order of things that, during hasty visits to the city, I often called on the eccentric Mr. Clark, and, as he had promised upon our first acquaintance, he seemed always glad to see and welcome me in his new office. The more I knew of him the more I liked him, but I think I never fully understood him. No one seemed to know him quite so well as that.

Once I had a little private talk regarding him with the senior of the firm for which he worked. Mr. Clark, just prior to my call, had gone to lunch—would be back in half an hour. Would I wait there in the office until his return? Certainly. And the chatty senior entertained me:—Queer fellow—Mr. Clark!—as his father was before him. Used to be a member of the firm—his father; in fact, founded the business—made a fortune at it—failed, for an unfortunate reason, and went "up the flume." Paid every dollar that he owed, however, sacrificing the very home that sheltered his wife and children—but never rallied. He had quite a family, then? Oh, yes; had a family—not a large one, but a bright one—only they all seemed more or less unfortunate. The father was unfortunate—very; and died so, leaving his wife and two boys—the older son much like the father—splendid business capacities, but lacked will—couldn't resist some things—even weaker than the father in that regard, and died at half his age. But the younger brother—our Mr. Clark—remained, and he was sterling—"straight goods" in all respects. Lived with his mother—was her sole support. A proud woman, Mrs. Clark—a proud woman, with a broken spirit—withdrawn entirely from the world, and had been so for years and years. The Clarks, as had been mentioned, were all peculiar—even the younger Mr. Clark, our friend, I had doubtless noticed was an odd genius, but he had stamina—something solid about him, for all his eccentricities—could be relied upon. Had been with the house there since a boy of twelve—took him for the father's sake; had never missed a day's time in any line of work that ever had been given in his charge—was weakly-looking, too. Had worked his way from the cellar up—from the least pay to the highest—had saved enough to buy and pay for a comfortable house for his mother and himself, and, still a lad, maintained the expense of companion, attendant and maid-servant for the mother. Yet, with all this burden on his shoulders, the boy had worried through some way, with a jolly smile and a good word for every one. "A boy, sir," the enthusiastic senior concluded— "a boy, sir, that never was a boy, and never had a taste of genuine boyhood in his life—no more than he ever took a taste of whiskey, and you couldn't get that in him with a funnel!"

ECCENTRIC MR. CLARK

At this juncture Mr. Clark himself appeared, and in a particularly happy frame of mind. For an hour the delighted senior and myself sat laughing at the fellow's quaint conceits and witty sayings, the conversation at last breaking up with an abrupt proposition from Mr. Clark that I remain in the city overnight and accompany him to the theatre, an invitation I rather eagerly accepted. Mr. Clark, thanking me, and pivoting himself around on his high stool, with a mechanical "Good afternoon!" was at once submerged in his books, while the senior, following me out and stepping into a carriage that stood waiting for him at the curb, waved me adieu, and was driven away. I turned my steps up street, but remembering that my friend had fixed no place to meet me in the evening, I stepped back into the store-room and again pushed open the glass door of the office.

Mr. Clark still sat on the high stool at his desk, his back toward the door, and his ledger spread out before him.

"Mr. Clark!" I called.

He made no answer.

"Mr. Clark!" I called again, in an elevated key.

He did not stir.

I paused a moment, then went over to him, letting my hand drop lightly on his arm.

Still no response. I only felt the shoulder heave, as with a long-drawn quavering sigh, then heard the regular though labored breathing of a weary man that slept.

I had not the heart to waken him; but, lifting the still moistened pen from his unconscious fingers, I wrote where I might be found at eight that evening, folded and addressed the note, and, laying it on the open page before him, turned quietly away.

"Poor man!" I mused, compassionately, with a touch of youthful sentiment affecting me.—"Poor man! Working himself into his very grave, and with never a sign or murmur of complaint—worn and weighed down with the burden of his work, and yet with a nobleness of spirit and resolve that still conceals behind glad smiles and laughing words the cares that lie so heavily upon him!"

The long afternoon went by at last, and evening came; and, as promptly as my note requested, the jovial Mr. Clark appeared, laughing heartily, as we walked off down the street, at my explanation of the reason I had written my desires instead of verbally addressing him; and laughing still louder when I told him of my fears that he was overworking himself.

"Oh, no, my friend," he answered, gayly; "there's no occasion for anxiety on that account.—But the fact is, old man," he went on, half apologetically, "the fact is, I haven't been so overworked, of late, as over-wakeful. There's something in the night, I think, that does it. Do you know that the night is a great mystery to me —a great mystery! And it seems to be growing on me all the time. There's the trouble. The night to me is like some vast, incomprehensible being. When I write the name 'night' I instinctively write it with a capital. And I like my nights deep, and dark and swarthy, don't you know. Now some like clear and starry nights, but they're too pale for me—too weak and fragile altogether! They're popular with the masses, of course, these blue-eyed, golden-haired, 'moonlight-on-the-lake' nights; but, someway, I don't 'stand in' with them. My favorite night is the pronounced brunette—the darker the better. To-night is one of my kind, and she's growing more and more like it all the time. If it were not for depriving you of the theatre, I'd rather just drift off now in the deepening gloom till swallowed up in it—lost utterly. Come with me, anyhow!"

"Gladly," I answered, catching something of his own enthusiasm; "I myself prefer it to the play."

"I heartily congratulate you on your taste," he said, diving violently for my hand and wringing it. "Oh, it's going to be grimly glorious!—a depth of darkness one can wade out into, and knead it in his hands like dough!" And he laughed, himself, at this grotesque conceit.

And so we walked—for hours. Our talk—or, rather, my friend's talk—lulled and soothed at last into a calmer flow, almost solemn in its tone, and yet fretted with an occasional wildness of utterance and expression.

Half consciously I had been led by my companion, who for an hour had been drawing closer to me as we walked. His arm, thrust through my own, clung almost affectionately. We were now in some strange suburb of the city, evidently, too, in a low quarter, for from the windows of such business rooms and shops as bore any evidence of respectability the lights had been turned out and the doors locked for the night. Only a gruesome green light was blazing in a little drug-store just opposite, while at our left, as we turned the corner, a tumble-down saloon sent out upon the night a mingled sound of clicking billiard-balls, discordant voices, the harsher raspings of a violin, together with the sullen plunkings of a banjo.

"I must leave you here for a minute," said my friend, abruptly breaking a long silence, and loosening my arm. "The druggist over there is a patron of our house, and I am reminded of a little business I have with him. He is about closing, too, and I'll see him now, as I may not

be down this way again soon. No; you wait here for me
—right here," and he playfully but firmly pushed me
back, ran across the street, and entered the store.
Through the open door I saw him shake hands with the
man that stood behind the counter, and stand talking in
the same position for some minutes—both still clasping
hands, as it seemed; but as I mechanically bent with
closer scrutiny, the druggist seemed to be examining the
hand of Mr. Clark and working at it, as though picking
at a splinter in the palm—I could not quite determine
what was being done, for a glass show-case blurred an
otherwise clear view of the arms of both from the elbows
down. Then they came forward, Mr. Clark arranging
his cuffs, and the druggist wrapping up some minute
article he took from an upper show-case, and handing it
to my friend, who placed it in the pocket of his vest and
turned away. At this moment my attention was withdrawn by an extra tumult of jeers and harsh laughter in
the saloon, from the door of which, even as my friend
turned from the door opposite, a drunken woman reeled,
and, staggering round the corner as my friend came up,
fell violently forward on the pavement, not ten steps in
our advance. Instinctively, we both sprang to her aid,
and, bending over the senseless figure, peered curiously
at the bruised and bleeding features. My friend was

trembling with excitement. He clutched wildly at the limp form, trying, but vainly, to lift the woman to her feet. "Why don't you take hold of her?" he whispered, hoarsely. "Help me with her—quick! quick! Lift her up!" I obeyed without a word, though with a shudder of aversion as a drop of hot blood stung me on the hand.

"Now draw her arm about your shoulder—this way—and hold it so! And now your other arm around her waist—quick, man, quick, as you yourself will want God's arm about you when you fail! Now, come!" And with no other word we hurried with our burden up the empty darkness of the street.

I was utterly bewildered with it all, but something kept me silent. And so we hurried on, and on, and on, our course directed by my now wholly reticent companion. Where he was going, what his purpose was, I could but vaguely surmise. I only recognized that his intentions were humane, which fact was emphasized by the extreme caution he took to avoid the two or three late pedestrians that passed us on our way as we stood crowded in concealment—once behind a low shed, once in an entry-way; and once, at the distant rattle of a police whistle, we hurried through the blackness of a narrow alley into the silent street beyond. And on up this we passed, until at last we paused at the gateway of a cottage on our left. On to the door of that we went, my friend first violently jerking the bell, then opening the door with a night-key, and with me lifting the still senseless woman through the hall into a dimly lighted room upon the right, and laying her upon a clean white bed that glimmered in the corner. He reached and turned the gas on in a flaring jet, and as he did so, "This is my home," he whispered, "and this woman is —my mother!" He flung himself upon his knees beside her as he spoke. He laid his quivering lips against the white hair and the ruddy wound upon the brow; then dappled with his kisses the pale face, and stroked and petted and caressed the faded hands. "O God!" he moaned, "if I might only weep!"

The steps of some one coming down the stair aroused him. He stepped quickly to the door, and threw it open. It was a woman-servant. He simply pointed to the form upon the bed.

"Oh, sir!" exclaimed the frightened woman, "what has happened? What has happened to my poor, dear mistress?"

"Why did you let her leave the house?"

"She sent me away, sir. I never dreamed that she was going out again. She told me she was very sleepy and wanted to retire, and I helped her to undress before

I went. But she ain't bad hurt, is she?" she continued, stooping over the still figure and tenderly smoothing back the dishevelled hair.—"It's only the cheek bruised and the forehead cut a little—it's the blood that makes it look like a bad hurt. See, when I bathe it, it is not a bad hurt, sir. She's just been—she's just worn out, poor thing—and she's asleep—that's all."

He made no answer to the woman's speech, but turned toward me. "Five doors from here," he said, "and to your left as you go out, you will find the residence of Dr. Worrel. Go to him for me, and tell him he is wanted here at once. Tell him my mother is much worse. He will understand. I would go myself, but must see about arranging for your comfort upon your return, for you will not leave me till broad daylight—you must not!" I bowed in silent acceptance of his wishes, and turned upon my errand.

Fortunately, the doctor was at home, and returned at once with me to my friend, where, after a careful examination of his patient, he assured the anxious son that the wounds were only slight, and that her unconscious condition was simply "the result of over-stimulation, perhaps," as he delicately put it. She would doubtless waken in her usual rational state—an occurrence really more to be feared than desired, since her peculiar sensitiveness might feel too keenly the unfortunate happening. "Anyway," he continued, "I will call early in the morning, and, in the event of her awakening before that time, I will leave a sedative with Mary, with directions she will attend. She will remain here at her side. And as to yourself, Mr. Clark," the doctor went on, in an anxious tone, as he marked the haggard face and hollow eyes, "I insist that you retire. You must rest, sir—worrying for the past week as you have been doing is telling on you painfully. You need rest—and you must take it."

"And I will," said Mr. Clark, submissively. Stooping again, he clasped the sleeping face between his hands and kissed it tenderly. "Good night!" I heard him whisper—"good night—good night!" He turned, and, motioning for me to follow, opened the door—"Doctor, good night! Good night, Mary!"

He led the way to his own room up-stairs. "And now, my friend," he said, as he waved me to an easy-chair, "I have but two other favors to ask of you: The first is, that you talk to me, or read to me, or tell me fairy tales, or riddles—anything, so that you keep it up incessantly, and never leave off till you find me fast asleep. Then in the next room you will find a comfortable bed. Leave me sleeping here, and you sleep there. And the second favor," he continued, with a slow smile and an affected air of great deliberation—"oh, well, I'll not ask the second favor of you now. I'll keep it for you till tomorrow." And as he turned laughingly away and paced three or four times across the room, in his step, his gait, the general carriage of the figure, I was curiously reminded of the time, years before, that I had watched him from the door of the caboose, as he walked up the suburban street till the movement of the train had hidden him from view.

"Well, what will you do?" he asked, as he wheeled a cosey-cushioned lounge close beside my chair, and, removing his coat, flung himself languidly down.—"Will you talk or read to me?"

"I will read," I said, as I picked up a book to begin my vigil.

"Hold just a minute, then," he said, drawing a card and pencil from his vest.—"I may want to jot down a note or two.—Now, go ahead."

I had been reading in a low voice steadily for perhaps an hour, my companion never stirring from his first position, but although my eyes were never lifted from the book, I knew by the occasional sound of his pencil that he had not yet dropped asleep. And so, without a pause, I read monotonously on. At last he turned heavily. I paused. With his eyes closed he groped his hand across my knees and grasped my own. "Go on with the reading," he said, drowsily.—"Guess I'm going to sleep now—but you go right on with the story.— Good night!" His hand fumbled lingeringly a moment, then was withdrawn and folded with the other on his breast.

I read on in a lower tone an hour longer, then paused again to look at my companion. He was sleeping heavily, and although the features in their repose appeared unusually pale, a wholesome perspiration, as it seemed, pervaded all the face, while the breathing, though labored, was regular. I bent above him to lower the pillow for his head, and the movement half aroused him, as I thought at first, for he muttered something as though impatiently; but listening to catch his mutterings, I knew that he was dreaming. "It's what killed father," I heard him say. "And it's what killed Tom," he went on, in a smothered voice; "killed both—killed both! It sha'n't kill me; I swore it. I could bottle it—case after case —and never touch a drop. If you never take the first drink, you'll never want it. Mother taught me that. What made her ever take the first? Mother! mother! When I get to be a man, I'll buy her all the fine things she used to have when father was alive. Maybe I can buy back the old home, with the roses up the walk and the sunshine slanting in the hall."

And so the sleeper murmured on. Sometimes the voice was thick and discordant, sometimes low and clear and tuneful as a child's. "Never touch whiskey!" he went on, almost harshly. "Never—never! never! Drop in the street first. I did. The doctor will come then, and he knows what you want. Not whiskey.—Medicine; the kind that makes you warm again—makes you want to live; but don't ever dare touch whiskey. Let other people drink it if they want it. Sell it to them; they'll get it anyhow; but don't you touch it! It killed your father, it killed Tom, and—oh!—Mother! mother! mother!" Tears actually teemed from underneath the sleeper's lids, and glittered down the pallid and distorted features. "There's a medicine that's good for you when you want whiskey," he went on.—"When you are weak, and everybody else is strong—and always when the flagstones give way beneath your feet, and the long street undulates and wavers as you walk; why, that's a sign for you to take that medicine—and take it quick! Oh, it will warm you till the little pale-blue streaks in your white hands will bulge out again with tingling blood, and it will start up from its stagnant pools and leap from vein to vein till it reaches your being's furthest height and droops and falls and folds down over icy brow and face like a soft veil moistened with pure warmth. Ah! it is so deliriously sweet and restful!"

I heard a moaning in the room below, and then steps on the stairs, and a tapping at the door. It was Mary. Mrs. Clark had awakened and was crying for her son. "But we must not waken him," I said. "Give Mrs. Clark the medicine the doctor left for her—that will quiet her."

"But she won't take it, sir. She won't do anything at all for me—and if Mr. Clark could only come to her, for just a minute, she would—"

The woman's speech was broken by a shrill cry in the hall, and then the thud of naked feet on the stairway. "I want my boy—my boy!" wailed the hysterical woman from without.

"Go to your mistress—quick," I said, sternly, pushing the maid from the room.—"Take her back; I will come down to your assistance in a moment." Then I turned hastily to see if the sleeper had been disturbed by the woman's cries; but all was peaceful with him yet; and so, throwing a coverlet over him, I drew the door to silently and went below.

I found the wretched mother in an almost frenzied

state, and gathering in a violence that alarmed me to that extent I thought it best to again summon the physician; and bidding the servant not to leave her for an instant, I hurried for the help so badly needed. This time the doctor was long delayed, although he joined me with all possible haste, and with all speed accompanied me back to the unhappy home. Entering the door, our ears were greeted with a shriek that came piercing down the hall till the very echoes shuddered as with fear. It was the patient's voice shrilling from the sleeper's room up-stairs:—"O God! My boy! my boy! I want my boy, and he will not waken for me!" An instant later we were both upon the scene.

The woman in her frenzy had broken from the servant to find her son. And she had found him.

She had wound her arms about him, and had dragged his still sleeping form upon the floor. He would not waken, even though she gripped him to her heart and shrieked her very soul out in his ears. He would not waken. The face, though whiter than her own, betokened only utter rest and peace. We drew her, limp and voiceless, from his side. "We are too late," the doctor whispered, lifting with his finger one of the closed lids, and letting it drop to again.—"See here!" He had been feeling at the wrist; and, as he spoke, he slipped the sleeve up, baring the sleeper's arm. From wrist to elbow it was livid purple, and pitted and scarred with minute wounds—some scarcely sealed as yet with clotted blood.

"In heaven's name, what does it all mean?" I asked.

"Morphine," said the doctor, "and the hypodermic. And here," he exclaimed, lifting the other hand—"here is a folded card with your name at the top."

I snatched it from him, and I read, written in faint but rounded characters:

"I like to hear your voice. It sounds kind. It is like a far-off tune. To drop asleep, though, as I am doing now, is sweeter music—but read on.—I have taken something to make me sleep, and by mistake I have taken too much; but you will read right on. Now, mind you, this is not suicide, as God listens to the whisper of this pencil as I write! I did it by mistake. For years and years I have taken the same thing. This time I took too much—much more than I meant to—but I am glad. This is the second favor I would ask: Go to my employers to-morrow, show them this handwriting, and say I know for my sake they will take charge of my affairs and administer all my estate in the best way suited to my mother's needs. Good-bye, my friend—I can only say 'good night' to you when I shall take your hand an instant later and turn away forever."

Through tears I read it all, and ending with his name in full, I turned and looked down on the face of this man that I had learned to love, and the full measure of his needed rest was with him; and the rainy day that glowered and drabbled at the eastern windows of the room was as drearily stared back at by a hopeless woman's dull, demented eyes.

"THE BOY FROM ZEENY"

"THE BOY FROM ZEENY"

His advent in our little country town was at once abrupt and novel. Why he came, when he came, or how he came, we boys never knew. My first remembrance of him is of his sudden appearance in the midst of a game of "Ant'ny-over," in which a dozen boys besides myself were most enthusiastically engaged. The scene of the exciting contest was the centre of the main street of the town, the elevation over which we tossed the ball being the skeleton remains of a grand triumphal arch, left as a sort of cadaverous reminder of some recent political demonstration. Although I recall the boy's external appearance upon that occasion with some vagueness, I vividly remember that his trousers were much too large and long, and that his heavy, flapping coat was buttonless, and very badly worn and damaged at the sleeves and elbows. I remember, too, with even more distinctness, the hat he wore: it was a high, silk, bell-crowned hat—a man's hat and a veritable "plug"—not a new and shiny "plug," by any means, but still of dignity and gloss enough to furnish a noticeable contrast to the other appertainments of its wearer's wardrobe. In fact, it was through this latter article of dress that the general attention of the crowd came at last to be particularly drawn to its unfortunate possessor, who, evidently directed by an old-time instinct, had mechanically thrust the inverted "castor" under a falling ball, and the ball, being made of yarn wrapped tightly over a green walnut, and dropping from an uncommon height, had gone through the hat like a round shot.

Naturally enough, much merriment was occasioned by the singular mishap, and the victim of the odd occurrence seemed himself inclined to join in the boisterous laughter and make the most of his ridiculous misfortune. He pulled the hat back over his tousled head, and with the flapping crown of it still clinging by one frayed hinge, he capered into a grotesquely executed jig that made the clamorous crowd about him howl again.

"Wo! what a hat!" cried Billy Kinzey, derisively, and with a palpably rancorous twinge of envy in his heart; for Billy was the bad boy of our town, and would doubtless have enjoyed the strange boy's sudden notoriety in thus being able to convert disaster into positive fun.

"THE BOY FROM ZEENY"

"Wo! what a hat!" reiterated Billy, making a feint to knock it from the boy's head as the still capering figure pirouetted past him.

The boy's eye caught the motion, and he whirled suddenly in a backward course and danced past his reviler again, this time much nearer than before. "Better try it," he said, in a low, half-laughing tone that no one heard but Billy and myself. He was out of range in an instant, still laughing as he went.

"Durn him!" said Billy, with stifling anger, clutching his fist and leaving one knuckle protruding in a very wicked-looking manner.—"Durn him! He better not sass me! He's afeard to come past here ag'in and say that! I'll knock his durn ole 'stove-pipe' in the middle o' nex' week!"

"You will, hey?" queried a revolving voice, as the boy twirled past again—this time so near that Billy felt his taunting breath blown in his face.

' Yes, I 'will, hey'!" said Billy, viciously; and with a side-sweeping, flat-handed lick that sounded like striking a rusty sheet of tin, the crownless "plug" went spinning into the gutter, while, as suddenly, the assaulted little stranger, with a peculiarly pallid smile about his lips and an electric glitter in his eye, adroitly flung his left hand forward, smiting his insulter such a blow in the region of the brow that the unguarded Billy went tumbling backward, his plucky assailant prancing wildly around his prostrate form.

"Oh! come and see me!" snarled the strange boy, in a contemptuous tone, cocking his fists up in a scientific manner, and dropping into a stoop-shouldered swagger that would have driven envy into the heart of a bullying hack-driver. "Git the bloke on his pins!" he sneered, turning to the crowd.—"S'pose I'm goin' to hit a man w'en he's down?"

But his antagonist needed no such assistance. Stung with his unlooked-for downfall, bleeding from the first blow ever given him by mortal boy, and goaded to absolute frenzy by the taunts of his swaggering enemy, Billy sprang to his feet, and a moment later had succeeded in closing with the boy in a rough-and-tumble fight, in which his adversary was at disadvantage, being considerably less in size, hampered, too, with his loose, unbuttoned coat and baggy trousers. But, for all, he did some very efficient work in the way of a deft and telling blow or two upon the nose of his overpowering foe, who sat astride of his wriggling body, but wholly unable to get in a lick.

"Durn you!" said Billy, with his hand gripping the boy's throat, "holler 'nough!"

"THE BOY FROM ZEENY"

"Holler nothin'!" gurgled the boy, with his eyes fairly starting from his head.

"Oh, let him up, Billy," called a compassionate voice from the excited crowd.

"Holler 'nough and I will," said Billy, in a tragic whisper in the boy's ear. "Durn ye! holler 'Calf-rope!'"

The boy only shook his head, trembled convulsively, let fall his eyelids, and lay limp and, to all appearances, unconscious.

The startled Billy loosed his hold, rose half-way to his feet, then fiercely pounced again at his rival.

But it was too late.—The ruse had succeeded, and the boy was once more on his feet.

"You fight like a dog!" said the strange boy, in a tone of infinite contempt—"and you *air* a dog! Put up yer props like a man and come at me, and I'll meller yer head till yer mother won't know you! Come on! I dare you!"

This time, as Billy started forward at the challenge, I regret to say that in his passion he snatched up from the street a broken buggy-spoke, before which warlike weapon the strange boy was forced warily to retreat. Step by step he gave back, and step by step his threatening foe advanced. I think, perhaps, part of the

"THE BOY FROM ZEENY"

strange boy's purpose in thus retreating was to arm himself with one of the "axe-handles" that protruded from a churn standing in front of a grocery, toward which he slowly backed across the sidewalk. However that may be, it is evident he took no note of an open cellar-way that lay behind him, over the brink of which he deliberately backed, throwing up his hands as he disappeared.

We heard a heavy fall, but heard no cry. Some loungers in the grocery, attracted by the clamor of the throng without, came to the door inquiringly; one man, learning what had happened, peered down the stairway of the cellar, and called to ask the boy if he was hurt, which query was answered an instant later by the appearance of the boy himself, his face far whiter than his shirt, and his lips trembling, but his teeth clinched.

"Guess I broke my arm ag'in," he said, briefly, as the man leaned over and helped him up the steps, the boy sweeping his keen eyes searchingly over the faces of the crowd. "It's the *right* arm, though," he continued, glancing at the injured member dangling helplessly at his side—"*this-'un's* all right yet!" and as he spoke he jerked from the man's assistance, wheeled round, and an instant later, as a buggy-spoke went hurtling through the air, he slapped the bewildered face of Billy with his open hand. "Dam' coward!" he said.

"THE BOY FROM ZEENY"

Then the man caught him, and drew him back, and the crowd closed in between the combatants, following, as the boy with the broken arm was hurried down street to the doctor's office, where the door was immediately closed on the rabble and all the mystery within—not an utter mystery, either, for three or four enterprising and sagacious boys slipped off from the crowd that thronged in front, and, climbing by a roundabout way and over a high board-fence into the back yard, secretly posted themselves at the blinded window in the rear of the little one-roomed office and breathlessly awaited advices from within.

"They got him laid out on the settee," whispered a venturous boy who had leaned a board against the window-sill and climbed into a position commanding the enviable advantage of a broken window-pane. "I kin see him through a hole in the curtain. Keep still!

"They got his coat off, and his sleeve rolled up," whispered the boy, in continuation—"and the doctor's a-givin' him some medicine in a tumbler. Now he's a-pullin' his arm. Gee-mun-nee! I kin hear the bones crunch!"

"Hain't he a-cryin'?" queried a milk-faced boy, with very large blue eyes and fine white hair, and a grieved expression as he spoke.—"Hain't he a-cryin'?"

"THE BOY FROM ZEENY"

"Well, he hain't!" said the boy in the window, with unconscious admiration. "Listen!

"I heerd him thist tell 'em 'at it wasn't the first time his arm was broke. Now keep still!" and the boy in the window again bent his ear to the broken pane.

"He says both his arms's be'n broke," continued the boy in the window—"says this-'un 'at's broke now's be'n broke two times 'fore this time."

"Dog-gone! hain't he a funny feller!" said the milk-faced boy, with his big eyes lifted wistfully to the boy in the window.

"He says onc't his pap broke his arm w'en he was whippin' him," whispered the boy in the window.

"Bet his pa's a wicked man!" said the milk-faced boy, in a dreamy, speculative way—"s'pect he's a drunkard, er somepin'!"

"Keep still!" said the boy at the window; "they're tryin' to git him to tell his pap's name and his, and he won't do it, 'cause he says his pap comes and steals him ever' time he finds out where he is."

The milk-faced boy drew a long, quavering breath and gazed suspiciously round the high board-fence of the enclosure.

"He says his pap used to keep a liberty-stable in Zeeny—in Ohio somers,—but he daresn't stay round *there* no more, 'cause he broke up there, and had to skedaddle er they'd clean him out! He says he hain't got no mother, ner no brothers, ner no sisters, ner no nothin'—on'y," the boy in the window added, with a very dry and painful swallow, "he says he hain't got nothin' on'y thist the clothes on his back!"

"Yes, and I bet," broke in the milk-faced boy, abruptly, with his thin lips compressed, and his big eyes fixed on space—"yes, and I bet he kin lick Bill Kinzey, ef his arm *is* broke!"

At this juncture some one inside coming to raise the window, the boy at the broken pane leaped to the ground, and, flocking at his heels, his frightened comrades bobbed one by one over the horizon of the high fence and were gone in an instant.

So it was that the hero of this sketch came to be known as "The Boy from Zeeny."

The Boy from Zeeny, though evidently predisposed to novel and disastrous happenings, for once, at least, had come upon a streak of better fortune; for the doctor, it appeared, had someway taken a fancy to him, and had offered him an asylum at his own home and hearth—the compensation stipulated, and suggested by the boy himself, being a conscientious and efficient service in the doctor's stable. Even with his broken arm splinted

"THE BOY FROM ZEENY"

and bandaged and supported in a sling, The Boy from Zeeny could be daily seen loping the doctor's spirited horse up the back alley from the stable to the office, with the utter confidence and careless grace of a Bedouin. When, at last, the injured arm was wholly well again, the daring feats of horsemanship of which the boy was capable were listened to with incredulity by the "good" boys of the village school, who never played "hookey" on long summer afternoons, and, in consequence, never had a chance of witnessing The Boy from Zeeny loping up to the "swimmin'-hole," a mile from town, barebacked, with nothing but a halter, and his face turned toward the horse's tail. In fact, The Boy from Zeeny displayed such a versatility of accomplishments, and those, too, of a character but faintly represented in the average boy of the country town, that, for all the admiration their possessor evoked, an equal envy was aroused in many a youthful breast.

"The boys in this town's down on you!" said a cross-eyed, freckle-faced boy, one day, to The Boy from Zeeny.

The Boy from Zeeny was sitting in the alley window of the hay-loft of the doctor's stable, and the cross-eyed boy had paused below, and, with his noward-looking eyes upturned, stood waiting the effect of this intelligence.

"THE BOY FROM ZEENY"

"What do I care fer the boys in this town?" said The Boy from Zeeny.

"The boys in this town," repeated the cross-eyed boy, with a slow, prophetic flourish of his head—"the boys in this town says 'cause you come from Zeeny and blacked Bill Kinzey's eye, 'at you think you're goin' to run things round here! And you'll find out you ain't the bosst o' this town!" and the cross-eyed boy shook his head again with dire foreboding.

"Looky here, Cocky!" said The Boy from Zeeny, trying to focus a direct gaze on the boy's delusive eyes, "w'y don't you talk straight out from the shoulder? I reckon 'the boys in this town,' as you call 'em, didn't send *you* round here to tell me w'at *they* was goin' to do! But ef you want to take it up fer 'em, and got any sand to back you, jest say it, and I'll come down there and knock them durn twisted eyes o' yourn straight ag'in!"

"Yes, you will!" muttered the cross-eyed boy, with dubious articulation, glancing uneasily up the alley.

"What?" growled The Boy from Zeeny, thrusting one dangling leg farther out the window, supporting his weight by the palms of his hands, and poised as though about to spring—"w'at 'id you say?"

"Didn't say nothin'," said the cross-eyed boy, feebly; and then, as a sudden and most bewildering smile lit up

"THE BOY FROM ZEENY"

his defective eyes, he exclaimed: "Oh! I tell you what le's do! Le's me and you git up a show in your stable, and don't let none o' the other boys be in it! I kin turn a handspring like you, and purt' nigh walk on my hands; and you kin p'form on the slack-rope—and spraddle out like the 'inja-rubber man'—and hold a pitchfork on yer chin—and stand up on a horse 'ithout a-holdin'—and—and—Oh! ever'thing!" And as the cross-eyed boy breathlessly concluded this list of strong attractions, he had The Boy from Zeeny so thoroughly inoculated with the enterprise that he warmly closed with the proposition, and the preparations and the practice for the show were at once inaugurated.

Three hours later, an extremely cross-eyed boy, with the freckles of his face thrown into vivid relief by an intense pallor, rushed pantingly into the doctor's office with the fateful intelligence that The Boy from Zeeny had "fell and broke his arm ag'in." And this time, as it seemed, the hapless boy had surpassed the seriousness of all former fractures, this last being of a compound nature, and very painful in the setting, and tedious in recovery; the recovery, too, being anything but perfect, since it left the movement of the elbow somewhat restricted, and threw the little fellow's arm in an unnatural position, with the palm of the hand turned forward as he walked. But for all that, the use of it was, to all appearances, but little impaired.

Doubtless it was through such interludes from rough service as these accidents afforded that The Boy from Zeeny had acquired the meagre education he possessed. The doctor's wife, who had from the first been kind to him, grew to like him very much. Through her gentle and considerate interest he was stimulated to study by the occasional present of a simple volume. Oftentimes the good woman would devote an hour to his instruction in the mysteries of the book's orthography and rhetoric.

Nor was The Boy from Zeeny a dull pupil; neither was he an ungrateful one. He was quick to learn, and never prouder than when a mastered lesson gained for him the approbation of his patient instructor.

The history of The Boy from Zeeny, such as had been gathered by the doctor and his wife, was corroborative in outline with the brief hint of it as communicated to the curious listeners at the rear window of the doctor's office on the memorable day of the boy's first appearance in the town. He was without family, save a harsh, unfeeling father, who, from every evidence, must have neglected and abused the child most shamefully, the circumstantial proof of this fact being evidenced in the boy's frank acknowledgment that he had repeatedly "run away" from him, and his still firm resolve to keep his name a secret, lest he might thereby be traced to his present security and fall once more into the hands of his unnatural parent.

Certain it was that the interest of all who knew his story was in hearty sympathy with the lad, and when one morning it was rumored that The Boy from Zeeny had mysteriously disappeared, and the rumor rapidly developed into an unquestionable fact, there was a universal sense of regret in the little town, which in turn resolved itself into positive indignation when it was learned from the doctor that an explanation, printed in red keel on the back of a fragmental bit of circus-poster, had been found folded and tucked away in the buckle-strap of his horse's bridle. The somewhat remarkable communication, in sprawling capitals, ran thus:

"PAPS GOT ME AGIN. I HAF TO GO. DAM HIM. DOC TEL HER TO KEEP MY BOOCKS. GOOD BY. I FED OLE CHARLY. I FED HIM OTES AND HA AN CORN. HE WONT NEED NO MORE FER A WEAK. AN BRAND TO. DOC TEL HER GOOD BY."

It was a curious bit of composition—uncouth, assuredly, and marred, maybe, with an unpardonable profanity—but it served. In the silence and gloom of the

"THE BOY FROM ZEENY"

old stable, the doctor's fingers trembled as he read, and the good wife's eyes, peering anxiously above his heaving shoulder, filled and overflowed with tears.

I wish that it were in the veracious sequence of this simple history to give this wayward boy back to the hearts that loved him, and that still in memory enshrine him with affectionate regard; but the hapless lad—the little ragged twelve-year-old that wandered out of nowhere into town, and wandered into nowhere out again—never returned. Yet we who knew him in those old days—we who were children with him, and, in spite of boyish jealousies and petty bickerings, admired the gallant spirit of the lad—are continually meeting with reminders of him; the last instance of which, in my own experience, I cannot here refrain from offering:

For years I have been a wanderer from the dear old town of my nativity, but through all my wanderings a gracious fate has always kept me somewhere in its pleasant neighborhood, and, in consequence, I often pay brief visits to the scenes of my long-vanished boyhood. It was during such a visit, but a few short years ago, that remembrances of my lost youth were most forcibly recalled by the progress of the County Fair, which institution I was permitted to attend through the kindness of an old chum who drove me over in his buggy.

Although it was not the day for racing, we found the track surrounded by a dense crowd of clamorous and applausive people.

"What does it mean?" I asked my friend, as he guided his horse in and out among the trees toward the edge of the enclosure.

"It's Professor Andrus, I suspect," he answered, rising in the buggy as he spoke, and peering eagerly above the heads of the surging multitude.

"And who's Professor Andrus?" I asked, striking a match against the tire of the now stationary buggy-wheel, and lighting the stump of my cigar.

"Why, haven't you heard of the famous Professor?" he answered, laughingly—immediately adding in a serious tone: "Professor Andrus is the famous 'horse-tamer' who has been driving the country absolutely wild here for two or three days. Stand up here where you can see!" he went on, excitedly.

"Yonder he comes! Isn't that splendid?"

And it was.

Across the sea of heads, and facing toward us down the track, I caught sight of a glossy span of horses that in their perfect beauty of symmetry, high heads, and tossing manes looked as though they were just prancing out of some Arabian dream. The animals seemed nude of rein or harness, save but a jewelled strap that crossed the breast of each, together with a slender trace at either side connecting with a jaunty little phaeton whose glittering wheels slivered the sunshine into splinters as they spun. Upon the narrow seat of the airy vehicle sat the driver. No lines were wound about his hands—no shout or lash to goad the horses to their telling speed. They were simply directed and controlled by the graceful motions of a long and slender whip which waved slowly to and fro above their heads. The great crowd cheered the master as he came. He arose deliberately, took off his hat, and bowed. The applause was deafening. Still standing, he whizzed past us and was gone. But something in the manner of the handsome fellow struck me with a strange sense of familiarity. Was it the utter disregard of fear that I saw within his face? Was it the keenness of the eye and the perfect self-possession of the man? Or was it—was it the peculiar way in which the right arm had dropped to his side after his salute to us while curving past us, and did I fancy, for that reason, that the palm of his hand turned forward as he stood?

"Clear the track, there!" came a far voice across the ring.—"Don't cross there, in God's name! Drive back!"

The warning evidently came too late. There was an instant's breathless silence, then a far-away, pent-sounding clash, then utter havoc in the crowd: The ropes about the ring were broken over, and a tumultuous tide of people poured across the ring, myself borne on the very foremost wave.

"Jist the buggy smashed, that's all!" cried a voice. "The hosses hain't hurt—ner the man."

The man referred to was the Professor. I caught a glimpse of him as he rose from the grassy bank where he had been flung. He was very pale, but calm. An uncouth man brought him his silk hat from where it had rolled in the dust.

"Wish you'd just take this handkerchief and brush it off," said the Professor; "I guess I've broke my arm."

It was The Boy from Zeeny.

THE OLD MAN

THE OLD MAN

[*Response made to the sentiment, " The Old Man," at the annual dinner of the Indianapolis Literary Club.*]

"'You are old, Father William,' the young man said,
 'And your hair has become very white,
And yet you incessantly stand on your head—
 Do you think, at your age, it is right?'"

THE Old Man never grows so old as to become either stale, juiceless, or unpalatable. The older he grows, the mellower and riper he becomes. His eyes may fail him, his step falter, and his big-mouthed shoes—"A world too wide for his shrunk shanks"—may cluck and shuffle as he walks; his rheumatics may make great knuckles of his knees; the rusty hinges of his vertebræ may refuse cunningly to articulate, but all the same the "backbone" of the old man has been time-seasoned, tried, and tested, and no deerskin vest was ever buttoned round a tougher! Look at the eccentric kinks and curvings of it—its abrupt depression at the base, and its rounded bulging at the shoulders; but don't laugh at the smart young man who airily observes how full-chested the old man would be if his head were only turned around, and don't kill the young man, either, until you take him out some place and tell him that the old man got himself warped up in that shape along about the times when everybody had to hump himself. Try to bring before the young man's defective mental vision a dissolving view of a "good old-fashioned barn-raisin'"—and the old man doing all the "raisin'" himself, and "grubbin'," and "burnin'" logs and "underbrush," and "dreenin'" at the same time, and trying to coax something besides calamus to grow in the spongy little tract of swamp-land that he could stand in the middle of and "wobble" and shake the whole farm. Or, if you can't recall the many salient features of the minor disadvantages under which the old man used to labor, your pliant limbs may soon overtake him, and he will smilingly tell you of trials and privations of the early days, until your anxiety about the young man just naturally stagnates, and dries up, and evaporates, and blows away.

In this little side-show of existence the old man is always worth the full price of admission. He is not only the greatest living curiosity on exhibition, but the object

THE OLD MAN

of the most genial solicitude and interest to the serious observer. It is even good to look upon his vast fund of afflictions, finding prominent above them all that wholesome patience that surpasseth understanding; to dwell compassionately upon his prodigality of aches and ailments, and yet, by his pride in their wholesale possession, and his thorough resignation to the inevitable, to be continually rebuked, and in part made envious of the old man's right-of-title situation. Nature, after all, is kinder than unkind to him, and always has a compensation and a soothing balm for every blow that age may deal him. And in the fading embers of the old man's eyes there are, at times, swift flashes and rekindlings of the smiles of youth, and the old artlessness about the wrinkled face that dwelt there when his cheeks were like the pippins, and his

> "red lips, redder still,
> Kissed by strawberries on the hill."

And thus it is the children are intuitively drawn toward him, and young, pure-faced mothers are forever hovering about him, with just such humorings and kindly ministrations as they bestow upon the little emperor of the household realm, strapped in his high chair at the dinner-table, crying "Amen" in the midst of "grace," and

THE OLD MAN

ignoring the "substantials" of the groaning board, and at once insisting upon a square deal of the more "temporal blessings" of jelly, cake, and pie. And the old man has justly earned every distinction he enjoys. Therefore let him make your hearthstone all the brighter with the ruddy coal he drags up from it with his pipe and comfortably settles himself where, with reminiscent eyes, he may watch the curling smoke of his tobacco as it indolently floats, and drifts, and dips at last, and vanishes up the grateful flue. At such times, when a five-year-old, what a haven every boy has found between the old grandfather's knees! Look back in fancy at the faces blending there—the old man's and the boy's—and, with the nimbus of the smoke-wreaths round the brows, the gilding of the firelight on cheek and chin, and the rapt and far-off gazings of the eyes of both, why, but for the silver tinsel of the beard of one and the dusky elf-locks of the other, the faces seem almost like twins.

With such a view of age, one feels like whipping up the lazy years and getting old at once. In heart and soul the old man is not old—and never will be. He is paradoxically old, and that is all. So it is that he grows younger with increasing years, until old age at worst is always at a level par with youth. Who ever saw a man so old as not secretly and most heartily to wish the

THE OLD MAN

veteran years upon years of greater age? And at what great age did ever any old man pass away and leave behind no sudden shock, and no selfish hearts still to yearn after him and grieve on unconsoled? Why, even in the slow declining years of old Methuselah—the banner old man of the universe,—so old that history grew absolutely tired waiting for him to go off some place and die—even Methuselah's taking off must have seemed abrupt to his immediate friends, and a blow to the general public that doubtless plunged it into the profoundest gloom. For nine hundred and sixty-nine years this durable old man had "smelt the rose above the mould," and doubtless had a thousand times been told by congratulative friends that he didn't look a day older than nine hundred and sixty-eight; and necessarily, the habit of living, with him, was hard to overcome. In his later years what an oracle he must have been, and with what reverence his friends must have looked upon the "little, glassy-headed, hairless man," and hung upon his every utterance! And with what unerring gift of prophecy could he foretell the long and husky droughts of summer—the gracious rains, at last,—the milk-sick breeding autumn and the blighting winter, simply by the way his bones felt after a century's casual attack of inflammatory rheumatism! And, having annually frosted his feet for some odd centuries—boy and man—we can fancy with what quiet delight he was wont to practise his prognosticating facilities on "the boys," forecasting the coming of the then fledgling cyclone and the gosling blizzard, and doubtless even telling the day of the month by the way his heels itched. And with what wonderment and awe must old chronic maladies have regarded him—tackling him singly or in solid phalanx, only to drop back pantingly, at last, and slink away dumfounded and abashed! And with what brazen pride the final conquering disease must have exulted over its shameless victory! But this is pathos here, and not a place for ruthless speculation: a place for asterisks—not words. Peace! peace! The man is dead! "The fever called living is over at last." The patient slumbers. He takes his rest. He sleeps. Come away! He is the oldest dead man in the cemetery.

Whether the hardy, stall-fed old man of the country, or the opulent and well-groomed old man of the metropolis, he is one in our esteem and the still warmer affections of the children. The old man from the country— you are always glad to see him and hear him talk. There is a breeziness of the woods and hills and a spice of the bottom-lands and thickets in everything he says, and dashes of shadow and sunshine over the waving wheat are in all the varying expressions of his swarthy face.

THE OLD MAN

The grip of his hand is a thing to bet on, and the undue loudness of his voice in greeting you is even lulling and melodious, since it unconsciously argues the frankness of a nature that has nothing to conceal. Very probably you are forced to smile, meeting the old man in town, where he never seems at ease, and invariably apologizes in some way for his presence, saying, perhaps, by way of explanation: "Yes-sir, here I am, in spite o' myse'f. Come in day afore yisterd'y. Boys was thrashin' on the place, and the beltin' kep' a-troublin' and delayin' of 'em —and I was potterin' round in the way anyhow, tel finally they sent me off to town to git some whang-luther and ribbets, and while I was in, I thought—I thought I'd jest run over and see the Jedge about that Henry County matter; and as I was knockin' round the court-house, first thing I knowed I'll be switched to death ef they didn't pop me on the jury! And here I am, eatin' my head off up here at the tavern. Reckon, tho', the County'll stand good fer my expenses. Ef hit cain't, I kin!" And, with the heartiest sort of a laugh, the old man jogs along, leaving you to smile till bedtime over the happiness he has unconsciously contributed.

Another instance of the old man's humor under trying circumstances was developed but a few days since. This old man was a German citizen of an inundated town in the Ohio valley. There was much of the pathetic in his experience, but the bravery with which he bore his misfortunes was admirable. A year ago his little home was first invaded by the flood, and himself and wife, and his son's family, were driven from it to the hills for safety —but the old man's telling of the story cannot be improved upon. It ran like this: "Last year, ven I svwim out fon dot leedle home off mine, mit my vife, unt my son his vife unt leedle girls, I dink dot's der last time goot-bye to dose proberty! But afder der vater it gone down, unt dry oop unt eberding, dere vas yet der house dere. Unt my friends dey sait, 'Dot's all you got yet— Vell, feex oop der house—dot's someding! feex oop der house, unt you vood still hatt yet a home!' Vell, all summer I go to work, unt spent me eberding unt feex der proberty. Den I got yet a morgage on der house! Dees time here der vater come again—till I vish it vas last year vonce! Unt now all I safe is my vife, unt my son his vife, unt my leedle granchilderns! Else everding is gone! All—everding!—Der house gone—unt—unt—der morgage gone, too!" And then the old Teutonic face "melted all over in sunshiny smiles," and, turning, he bent and lifted a sleepy little girl from a pile of dirty bundles in the depot waiting-room and went pacing up and down the muddy floor, saying cheery things in German to the child. I thought the whole thing rather beautiful. That's the kind of an old man who, saying good-bye to his son, would lean and kiss the young man's hand, as in the Dutch regions of Pennsylvania, two or three weeks ago, I saw an old man do.

Mark Lemon must have intimately known and loved the genteel old man of the city when the once famous domestic drama of "Grandfather Whitehead" was conceived. In the play the old man—a once prosperous merchant—finds a happy home in the household of his son-in-law. And here it is that the gentle author has drawn at once the poem, the picture, and the living proof of the old Wordsworthian axiom, "The child is father to the man." The old man, in his simple way, and in his great love for his wilful little grandchild, is being continually distracted from the grave sermons and moral lessons he would read the boy. As, for instance, aggrievedly attacking the little fellow's neglect of his books and his inordinate tendency toward idleness and play—the culprit, in the meantime, down on the floor clumsily winding his top—the old man runs on something in this wise:

"Play! play! play! Always play and no work, no study, no lessons. And here you are, the only child of the most indulgent parents in the world—parents that, proud as they are of you, would be ten times prouder only to see you at your book, storing your mind with useful knowledge, instead of, day in, day out, frittering away your time over your toys and your tops and marbles. And even when your old grandfather tries to advise you and wants to help you, and is always ready and eager to assist you, and all—why, what's it all amount to? Coax and beg and tease and plead with you, and yet—and yet"— (Mechanically kneeling as he speaks) "Now that's not the way to wind your top! How many more times will I have to show you!" And an instant later the old man's admonitions are entirely forgotten, and his artless nature—dull now to everything but the childish glee in which he shares—is all the sweeter and more lovable for its simplicity.

And so it is, Old Man, that you are always touching the very tenderest places in our hearts—unconsciously appealing to our warmest sympathies, and taking to yourself our purest love. We look upon your drooping figure, and we mark your tottering step and trembling hand, yet a reliant something in your face forbids compassion, and a something in your eye will not permit us to look sorrowfully on you. And, however we may smile at your quaint ways and old-school oddities of manner and of speech, our merriment is ever tempered with the gentlest reverence.